George Washington Moon

The Revisers' English

A Series of Criticisms, Showing the Revisers' Violations of the Laws of the Language

George Washington Moon

The Revisers' English
A Series of Criticisms, Showing the Revisers' Violations of the Laws of the Language

ISBN/EAN: 9783337085292

Printed in Europe, USA, Canada, Australia, Japan

Cover: Foto ©Lupo / pixelio.de

More available books at **www.hansebooks.com**

THE

REVISERS' ENGLISH.

With Photographs of the Revisers.

SERIES OF CRITICISMS, SHOWING THE REVISERS' VIOLATIONS
OF THE LAWS OF THE LANGUAGE.

BY

G. WASHINGTON MOON, F.R.S.L.

MEMBER OF THE COUNCIL OF THE ROYAL SOCIETY OF LITERATURE
AUTHOR OF "THE DEAN'S ENGLISH," ETC.

" Bad grammar is injustice to truth."
—*The* Rev. JOSEPH ANGUS, D.D.,
One of the Revisers.

LONDON:
HATCHARDS, PICCADILLY
1882.

Dedicated

TO THE MEMORY OF MY ANCESTOR,

THOMAS ALDAM,

OF WARMSWORTH, IN THE COUNTY OF YORK.

ONE OF THE EARLIEST MEMBERS

OF

"THE SOCIETY OF FRIENDS."

A good man, who died in peace with all men, and loving trust in God, A.D. 1660.

———o———

The Bible was to him his greatest treasure; and preaching its truths, his greatest delight. But he was persecuted, he was reviled, he was buffeted, he was spit upon, and for conscience' sake he suffered the spoiling of his goods, and endured years of cruel imprisonment. However, the knowledge of his own rectitude and of God's love sustained him through it all; and, on his release, being moved with sympathy for his companions in tribulation, he visited and condoled with them in the various prisons throughout the kingdom, and drew up a report of the wrongs and sufferings of his co-religionists, and personally laid it before Oliver Cromwell, and pleaded repeatedly, in the name of humanity and justice, that they might be liberated. His petition being finally rejected, he fearlessly denounced the Protector to his face for his tyranny, and predicted the downfall of his government.—See "Encyclopædia Britannica," 8th edition, vol. xviii., p. 718.

PREFACE.

I AM surprised to find myself, after a silence of fifteen years, again engaged in controversy on the Queen's English. I am not a lover of contention, but of peace. There was a time when I could say, " I delight in a wordy warfare with one who wields his weapon well;" but now, my joy is not in the unrest of battle, but in the restfulness of the Beautiful—the Beautiful in deed and in word.

It may be that it is my excessive love of the beautiful, which makes me so keenly sensitive to anything that mars it; and certainly it is the hope of preserving and perfecting that which is beautiful in our language that has impelled me to engage in the task of exposing the Revisers' errors in it in the New Testament—a task from which I should have shrunk, were it not that I regard the Bible as the Temple of God's Truth, and therefore a sacred sanctuary for the shrine of the Beautiful, the defence of which is incumbent upon every man.

The mind which allows itself complacently to delight in anything below the highest standard of excellence, is thereby dwarfing its faculties; for we become assimilated to that which we worship, and are ennobled or debased by the influence of that upon which our minds dwell with satisfaction. From this circumstance arises the necessity for aiming at perfection in all things; and if language is that which pre-eminently distinguishes man from the beasts, the attainment of perfection in language is worthy of our most studious efforts. Language is the vehicle of thought; and, in the Bible, it is the vehicle of God's thoughts; therefore, if perfection in language ought to be looked for anywhere, it ought to be looked for, and found, in the Bible. I have looked for it in our translation, and have not found it; hence these letters.

They were originally published, in conjunction with others from some of the Revisers themselves, in a series of consecutive numbers of *Public Opinion*, and drew forth counter-criticisms from certain university professors and learned theologians who sought to defend the Revisers from the charges of error which I had brought against them. Those counter-criticisms and the replies which they elicited have, I hope, rendered the letters entertaining as well as additionally instructive; for, as long as human nature is what it is, we cannot but be amused by the mistakes and misadventures of the wise.

G. W. M.

THE NEW TESTAMENT REVISERS,
1870-1880.

ANGUS, Dr. J., Principal of the Baptist College, Regent's Park, London.

BICKERSTETH, Dr. E. H., Dean of Lichfield.

BLAKESLEY, Dr. J. W., Dean of Lincoln.

BROWN, Dr. D., Professor of Divinity, Free Church College, Aberdeen.

EADIE, Dr. J., Professor of Biblical Literature and Exegesis to the United Presbyterian Church, Scotland.

ELLICOTT, Dr. C. J., Bishop of Gloucester and Bristol.

HORT, Dr. F. J. A., Hulsean Professor of Divinity, Cambridge.

HUMPHRY, Rev. W. G., Prebendary of St. Paul's.

KENNEDY, Dr. B. H., Canon of Ely, and Regius Professor of Greek, Cambridge.

LEE, Dr. W., Archdeacon of Dublin.

LIGHTFOOT, Dr. J. B., Bishop of Durham.

MILLIGAN, Dr. W., Professor of Divinity, Aberdeen.

MOBERLY, Dr. G., Bishop of Salisbury.

xii THE NEW TESTAMENT REVISERS.

MOULTON, Dr. W. F., Professor of Classics, Wesleyan College, Richmond.
NEWTH, Dr. S., Principal of New College, London.
PALMER, Rev. E., Archdeacon of Oxford.
ROBERTS, Dr. A., Professor of Humanity, St. Andrews.
SCOTT, Dr. R., Dean of Rochester.
SCRIVENER, Dr. F. H. A., Prebendary of Exeter.
SMITH, Dr. G. VANCE, Principal of the Presbyterian College, Carmarthen.
STANLEY, Dr. A. P., Dean of Westminster.
TRENCH, Dr. R. C., Archbishop of Dublin.
VAUGHAN, Dr. C. J., Dean of Llandaff.
WESTCOTT, Dr. B. F., Regius Professor of Divinity, Cambridge.
WORDSWORTH, Dr. C., Bishop of St. Andrews.

In addition to the foregoing there were originally Dean Alford and Bishop Wilberforce, who both, greatly to the sorrow of all, died during the Revision, and Dean Merivale, who resigned.

The Secretary to the New Testament Company was the Rev. John Troutbeck, M.A., one of the Minor Canons of Westminster Abbey.

CONTENTS.

A

"*Afterthought,*" 48
"*Age, Of,*" or "*Old,*" 133
"*Agree together,*" 110
"*All,*" 114, 117
"*All which,*" 33, 117
"*Alone*" for "*Only,*" 92, 93
"*Also,*" 131, 132
"*Alternative,*" 57, 77
"*Alway*" and "*Always,*" 106, 107
Ambiguity, 133
"*And,*" 4, 13, 14
"*Another,*" 121
"*Apparent,*" 118
"*Appear, It would,*" 118, 119
"*As-as,*" 126
"*Asleep*" and "*the rest,*" 112
Authority of example, 50, 51
"*Aught*" and "*Ought,*" 119

B

"*Backward*" and "*Backwards,*" 107
Blasphemy, 98, 99
"*Both,*" 113, 116
"*But,*" 121

C

"*Chiefest,*" 108, 109
"*Circumstances, Under no,*" 78, 100
"*Come*" for "*Go,*" 92, 123-125

D

"*Dilemma,*" 49, 77
Doxology in the Lord' Prayer, Error in the, 35

CONTENTS.

E

"*Each*," 114, 129
"*Either*," 113, 115, 129
Ellipses, 49
"*Ever* and ever," 105, 106
"*Every*," 114
"*Except*," 80, 94-97

F

"*Fallen*" lightning, 141
"*Fewer*," 100
"*Footstool of his feet*," 109, 110
"*Forth*," 20
"*Forward*" and "*Forwards*" 107
"*Frequent*" and "*Often*," 137, 138

G

"*Get on*" and "*Get off*," 125
"*Go on*" and "*Be off*," 125
"*Good*" for "*Bad*," 126
Grecisms, 33, 34

H

"*Had rather*," 135
Hypothesis, 86

I

Idiom, 33, 34, 38

"*If*," 67, 68, 71-73, 80-86, 94, 129
Incest, 24
"*Incipient*" and "*Insipient*," 98, 99
Infinitive mood, 89
Irish bull, An, 78, 98
"*It*" and "*Him*," 29

L

Laconic writing, 4
"*Less*" for "*Fewer*," 100
Literal translation, 12, 32, 87
Logic of grammar, 121, 122

M

Misogynist, 66

N

"*Name of*" a name, 129
"*Naught*," 114, 119
"*Neither*," 113, 115
"*Nor*," 115
"*Now, then!*" 125, 126

O

"*Often*" for "*Frequent*," 137, 138
"*Oftentimes*," 137, 138
"*Old*" for "*Years of age*," 133

"*Other*," 114, 120, 122
"*Outward*" and "*Outwards*," 107

P

Parentheses, 129
Pronouns and Verbs, their agreement, 29-31
Pronouns, 22-24, 55, 113
"*Propose*" for "*Purpose*," 91
"*Purpose*" and "*Propose*," 90, 91, 94

Q

"*Quick*" for "*Living*," 134, 135
"*Quickening*" for "*Life-giving*," 134, 135

R

"*Rather*," 135
Reservation, Mental, 49

S

"*Seem, It would*," 119
"*See-saw*," 136
"*Shall*" and "*Will*," 43, 44, 59
"*Shamefastness*," 138-140
"*Should*" for "*Would*," 129
"*So-as*" for "*As-as*," 126
"*Sons*" and "*Sun*," 111

"*Stolen*" and "*Stole away*," 112
Style, 143
Subjunctive mood, 67, 68, 72-74, 129
"*Subterfuge*," 102

T

Tautology, 99, 111
Tautophany, 111
"*That, that, that*," 110, 111
"*That*" and "*Which*," 28, 55, 56
"*Them which*" and "*Them that*," 56
"*Though*," 67, 69, 80-86, 94, 129
"*Thy*" and "*Thine*," 28
Translation, The essentials of a good, 3, 12, 53

U

"*Unless*," 67, 80, 94-97
"*Upward*" and "*Upwards*," 107

V

Verb, its agreement with the nominative, 8-11, 16-20, 35, 36, 46, 48, 51, 64, 65, 76, 77

CONTENTS.

Verb, the present tense to be used concerning things immutable, 45, 69

W

"*Whether*," 67, 74, 80–82
"*Who*" and "*Which*," 29, 56

"*Whole*," 116
"*Will*," the auxiliary, 41, 58-60, 89, 102
"*Will*," the verb "*to will*," 41, 58, 90, 102
"*Wilt*," and "*Willest*," 40, 60, 89, 102
"*Would*," 59, 60

THE REVISERS' ENGLISH.

LETTER I.

INTRODUCTORY.

To the 'Revision' Editor of "Public Opinion." *

Sir,—In a letter of mine in the *Times*, two or three years ago, I expressed a hope that the reverend scholars engaged upon the Revision of the Sacred Scriptures would publish a tentative edition of their work, with the object of eliciting criticism and such additional information as would enable them to render as nearly perfect as possible the version which should ultimately be issued to the public. The suggestion was obviously one which must have

* The Rev. T. H. L. Leary, D.C.L. Oxon.

commended itself to every unbiassed mind, and I assume that the Revisers have acted in accordance with it, and that this version of the New Testament is only preliminary to that which will finally be published "by authority."

Now, as the revelation of God belongs to us and to our children for ever (Deut. xxix. 29), it is the duty of every man, according to his ability, to assist in handing down to posterity a faithful and intelligent transcript of that revelation; and if he does so with a pure motive, all personal feeling will be subservient to the perfecting of the work; and, that being the case, no one will be more desirous than he that his own errors of interpretation or of language should be corrected; and, as no person can call in question the purity of motive of the Revisers, I do not fear that any one of them will be offended by the suggestions which, in the interest of truth, others will presume to offer for their consideration. Their love of the truth will outweigh all prejudice, and no adverse criticism will have the effect of disturbing their Christian equanimity:—"Great peace have they which love Thy law; and nothing shall offend them." (Psalm cxix. 165.)

Two things are essential to a good translation: the one, that it be a faithful expression of the ideas intended to be conveyed in the original; and the other, that it be a grammatical expression of those ideas, according to the idiom of the language into which the translation is to be made. The consideration of the former, in its relation to the present work, I leave to those scholars who have made Greek their special study; the consideration of the latter only I presume to take upon myself.

As the publication of the work is so recent, and I therefore have had but little time for its perusal, this, my first letter upon it, will be very short; but it must, I regret to say, contain the statement that the changes which have been made in the passages that I have read have created in my mind a profound

4   THE REVISERS' ENGLISH.

feeling of disappointment. I entertained a reasonable hope that no changes would be introduced but those which were absolutely indispensable, and I read in the Preface that it was resolved that the language of the Authorised Version should be adhered to as far as possible; but what necessity was there for the alterations which have been made in Matt. xiii. 37-39? As that passage stands in the Authorised Version it is one of the finest specimens of laconic writing to be found in the whole of the Bible. I will quote it, and side by side with it will quote the passage as altered in the Revised Version, that the lamentable weakness of the latter may be manifest.

Authorised Version.	*Revised Version.*
" Declare unto us the parable of the tares of the field.	" Explain unto us the parable of the tares of the field. *And* he answered *and* said, He that soweth the good seed is the Son of man; *and* the field is the world; *and* the good seed, *these* are the sons of the
" He answered and said unto them, " He that soweth the good seed is the Son of man :	
"The field is the world : the good seed are the chil-	

THE REVISERS' ENGLISH.

dren of the kingdom; but the tares are the children of the wicked one:

"The enemy that sowed them is the devil: the harvest is the end of the world; and the reapers are the angels."

kingdom; *and* the tares are the sons of the evil one; *and* the enemy that sowed them is the devil; *and* the harvest is the end of the world; *and* the reapers are angels."

[The italics are my own.]

The needless insertion of the conjunction "*and*" six additional times has utterly spoilt the passage, making it feeble in the extreme, without adding even one idea!—Yours faithfully,

G. WASHINGTON MOON.

LETTER II.

The Conjunction "and." *A Verb's agreement with its Nominative. Singular and Plural of Nouns.*

SIR,—One of the most difficult things which I have ever had to believe is that a company of the most eminent scholars in England, after ten and a half years of study, devoted to elucidating the meaning of the Sacred Scriptures, and to expressing that meaning in pure English, have deliberately issued to the world, as the result of so much thought, a work abounding with such errors as are to be found in the Revised Version of the New Testament, a copy of which now lies before me.

That there are among the Revisers some scholars eminent for the possession of a critical knowledge of their own language I know for a fact; but it is evident that they have so been in the minority that they have not been allowed to record, even in a foot-note, their protests against the grammatical errors of their colleagues in the work. I can only hope that those protests, which I am now endeavouring to re-echo, will be taken up by the Press, and that the voice of public remonstrance thus raised will, as with a mighty breath, sweep away from the sacred pages the dishonouring dust of error which the carelessness or the ignorance of man has suffered to rest there.

Having, in my previous letter, pointed out how one of the most graphic passages in the New Testament has been enfeebled by the needless insertion of the conjunction "*and*" six times in three consecutive verses, I continue my remarks upon the misuse of that part of speech, and shall show that the Revisers have actually treated it as if it were disjunctive instead of copulative; as if, in fact, it were the equivalent of its very opposite, the conjunction "*or*," and, therefore, as if it separated the parts of a sentence instead of uniting them.

One passage is as follows:—" Lay not up for yourselves treasures upon the earth, where moth *and* rust *doth* consume" (Matt. vi. 19). If it had been "where moth *or* rust," then "*doth*" would have been correct; but, as it is "where moth *and* rust," the nominative to the verb is plural, and therefore the verb also should have been plural; for it is one of the invariable rules of English grammar that the verb and its nominative must agree. The Revisers should have said, "Lay not up for yourselves treasures upon the earth, where moth and rust consume," not "*doth* consume," for that is saying "*they doth!*"

The law of the agreement between the nominative and the verb, which is one of the simplest in the language, has been strangely lost sight of in many passages, notwithstanding that every word in every passage in the New Testament has been the subject of deliberate consideration. The bewilderment which one feels in endeavouring to account for such errors surely justifies the expression of a hope that the learned scholars who have sanctioned the publication of those errors will explain to the world the reason of their existence.

In Matt. xxvii. 56, we read, " Among whom *was* Mary Magdalene, *and* Mary the mother of James and Joses, *and* the mother of the sons of Zebedee ; " *i.e.*, those three *was* among them ! This is culpable carelessness ; for, in the parallel passage in Mark xv. 40, it is said, " Among whom *were* both Mary Magdalene, and Mary the mother of James the less, and of Joses and Salome." If two Marys are plural, how can three Marys be singular ? I was going to say that it is a singular error, but, unfortunately, it is not so, for there are others like it ; see Acts xvii. 34, where it is said, " Among whom also *was* Dionysius the Areopagite, *and* a woman named Damaris, *and* others."

In Mark iii. 33, we read, "Who *is* my mother *and* my brethren?" Who *is* they! Carelessness again ; for, the parallel passage in Matt.

xii. 48, gives the inquiry grammatically, thus: "Who *is* my mother? and who *are* my brethren?" The Preface, p. xiv., says, respecting parallel passages, "Where, as in the case of the first three Evangelists, precisely the same clauses or sentences are found in more than one of the Gospels, it is necessary to translate them in every place in the same way."

In Rom. ix. 4, we read of the Israelites, "whose *is* the adoption, *and* the glory, *and* the covenants, *and* the giving of the law, *and* the service of God, *and* the promises." You see it says that all these things *is* theirs! Yet in the very next verse it correctly says, "whose *are* the fathers." How can these errors be explained? I confess that I am more than puzzled by them, when I reflect that the work is the result of ten years' study.

Again, in Eph. iii. 18, we read, "That ye may be strong to apprehend with all the saints what *is* the breadth *and* length *and* height *and* depth, and to know the love of Christ which passeth knowledge." It certainly passeth knowledge why the Revisers have sent forth such English as this. In the passage quoted there are four things mentioned; and the Revisers speak of our being strong to apprehend what *they is!* We should need to be "strong" indeed to "apprehend" why *they is* spoken of in this *singular* manner.— Yours faithfully,

G. WASHINGTON MOON.

LETTER III.

The Conjunction "and."

SIR, — As the Rev. A. Plummer, M.A., Master of University College, Durham,* attempts to justify the excessive use of the conjunction "*and*" in Matt. xiii. 37-39, on the ground of its equivalent being in the Greek text of that passage, I briefly revert to the subject to say that the first essential to a good translation, namely, " That it be a faithful expression of the *ideas* intended to be conveyed in the original," does not necessitate that the translation be *literal ;* and as the insertion of the conjunction "*and*" six additional times in the three verses does not make the passage one whit more faithful

* Rev. A. Plummer, M.A., is a Proctor and Tutor of the University of Durham, and late Fellow of Trinity College, Oxford, and Translator of ' Dr. Dollinger on Prophecy.'

to the expression of the original ideas, the Authorised Version of the passage is certainly preferable; for, whatever in a sentence does not add to its grace, its perspicuity, or its force, weakens it.

The foregoing example is not the only one of the kind, as the reader will see by referring to 1 Cor. xii. 8–10; where also there is the needless insertion of the conjunction "*and*" six times in three consecutive verses:—

Authorised Version.	*Revised Version.*
"To one is given, by the Spirit, the word of wisdom; to another the word of knowledge, by the same Spirit;	"To one is given through the Spirit the word of wisdom; *and* to another the word of knowledge, according to the same Spirit; to another faith, in the same Spirit; *and* to another gifts of healings in the one Spirit; *and* to another workings of miracles; *and* to another prophecy; *and* to another discernings of spirits; to another divers kinds of tongues; *and* to another the interpretation of tongues:"
"To another faith, by the same Spirit; to another the gifts of healing, by the same Spirit;	
"To another the working of miracles; to another prophecy; to another discernings of spirits; to another divers kinds of tongues; to another the interpretation of tongues:"	

No one can read these parallel passages and

hesitate to which to give the preference for terseness and graphic clearness of expression. Had the idea intended to be conveyed been the *number* of the operations of the Spirit, then the conjunction "*and*" would have added force to the statement; but the prominent idea is not that of number but of diversity—"*diversities* of gifts," "*diversities* of ministrations," "*diversities* of workings;" therefore, the "*and*" is worse than needless.

Now, in Heb. xi. 32 the idea of *number* is the prominent one, and there the conjunction "*and*" is essential to the enforcement of that idea, and in the Authorised Version very properly is inserted; but in the Revised Version it is thrice omitted, and its equivalent "*also*" is once omitted:—

Authorised Version.	*Revised Version.*
"And what shall I more say? for the time would fail me to tell of Gideon, *and* of Barak, *and* of Samson, *and* of Jephthae, of David *also*, *and* Samuel, *and* of the prophets."	"And what shall I more say? for the time will fail me if I tell of Gideon, Barak, Samson, Jephthah; of David and Samuel and the prophets."

Thus the Revisers have inserted the word where it was needless or worse than needless, and have omitted it where it was imperatively required!—Yours faithfully,

G. WASHINGTON MOON.

LETTER IV.

A Verb and its Nominative. Singular and Plural of Nouns. Things spoken of " severally."

SIR,—It is well known that when two parts of a sentence are united by the conjunction "*and*," and the nominative to the verb in the former part is singular, and the nominative in the latter part is plural, the verb must be repeated in the latter part, and be made in agreement with its nominative; otherwise the verb. in the singular will have to do duty for both nominatives, the plural as well as the singular; which, of course, would be grossly ungrammatical. The Revisers violated this rule, as I have shown in a previous letter, respecting Mark iii. 33, and they acted in conformity with it in Matt. xii. 48, and correctly wrote, " Who *is* my mother, and who *are* my brethren?" But in the very next chapter (Matt. xiii. 55), they wrote, with an inconsistency which, I am sorry to say, is not uncommon, "*Is* not his mother called Mary? and [*is* not] his brethren, James, and Joseph, and Simon, and Judas?" See also Rev. x. 1, "His face *was* as the sun, and his feet [*was*] as pillars of fire." The same error occurs in another form in Rev. xiii. 2, "His feet *were* as the feet of a bear, and his mouth [*were*] as the mouth of a lion."

The instances of non-agreement between the verb and its nominative, pointed out in my second letter, are only a few of those which might be adduced from the Revised Version of the New Testament, *e.g.*, "Where jealousy *and* faction *are*, there *is* confusion *and* every vile deed." (Jas. iii. 16.) If "jealousy and faction" are plural, how can "confusion and every vile deed" be singular? Moreover, if "jealousy and faction" are plural in Jas. iii. 16, why are "jealousy and strife" singular in 1 Cor. iii. 3?

Some one has very truly said that that in which mankind are most consistent is in their being inconsistent; and certainly the Revisers are not exceptions to the general rule.

In 1 Tim. i. 20, we read, "Of whom *is* Hymenæus *and* Alexander;" these evidently were *very singular* gentlemen, quite different from Phygelus *and* Hermogenes, spoken of in 2 Tim. i. 15, where we read, "Of whom *are* Phygelus *and* Hermogenes."

Again, in Matt. xxii. 40, we read, "On these two commandments hang*eth* the whole law, *and* the prophets," *i.e., they hangeth!* This is the more disgraceful, because, in the Authorised Version, the verb is correctly put in the plural: "On these two commandments *hang* all the law and the prophets." The term "*Revised*" is, when applied to this passage, unquestionably a misnomer.

The Revisers say in the Preface, p. xix., "We acted on the general principle of printing in italics words which did not appear to be necessarily involved in the Greek." That being so, the word "*was*," in Heb. ix. 4, is indisputably their own; and I ask them to explain its presence there. The passage is, " Wherein *was* a golden pot holding the manna, *and* Aaron's rod that budded, *and* the tables of the covenant," &c. These things *was* in it ! But, in verse 2 of the same chapter it says, "Wherein *were* the candlestick, *and* the table, *and* the shewbread."

Will the Revisers kindly tell me what there is peculiar about the connection of a pot, a rod, and the tables, that they unitedly should be singular, while a candlestick, a table, and the shewbread are plural ? Is the explanation of the anomaly to be found in the concluding words of the passage, where, respecting the pot, the rod, and the tables, it says, " Of which things we cannot now speak *severally*"?

In 1 Cor. xiii. 13, it says, "And now abid*eth* faith, hope, love, these three." If they are "*three*," why is not the verb plural ?

Once more: In James iii. 10, we read as follows:—" Out of the same mouth *cometh* forth blessing *and* cursing." To which I say, Doth they? And why have the Revisers inserted the word "*forth*," which is not in the Authorised Version, and is not needed, as the word "*out*" embodies it? The remainder of the verse—which I will take the liberty of addressing to the Revisers themselves, respecting the errors which I have exposed—forms a fitting conclusion to this letter, "My brethren, these things ought not so to be."—Yours faithfully,

G. WASHINGTON MOON.

LETTER V.

The Revisers' Errors—Their Source. Pronouns. A Strange Injunction: a Man to Marry his own Daughter.

SIR,—A medical friend of mine, with whom I was conversing about the anomalies in the English of the Revised New Testament, suggested, from the remembrance of an incident in his own experience, a not improbable explanation of them. He told me that, many years ago, during an examination, he was in great perplexity as to which of two ways of spelling a certain word was the correct one; and he hit upon the happy idea of spelling it in one way in one part of his paper, and in the other way in another part, thinking that, if the examiners found it correct in one place they would conclude that the other spelling, which of course would be incorrect, was simply a clerical error; and so they did, and he passed through his examination creditably.

This suggestion has really taken a load off my mind, for that the Revisers' errors were the effect either of carelessness or of ignorance was to me incomprehensible, and the happy idea that they may be accepted simply as evidences of doubt is a much more pleasing one, though how the Revisers could have been in doubt respecting any rule of the grammar of their own language is still a mystery; and if, in our investigations, we have occasionally to fall back on the hypothesis of carelessness as the cause of certain errors, it will, in the absence of any explanation from the Revisers themselves, at least be excusable.

Indeed, it was they who suggested the idea of carelessness; for, in their Preface, p. xvi., they say that they have been "*particularly careful*" as to the pronouns; thereby implying that they had not been so careful about the other parts of speech. The passage is as follows: "As to the pronouns and the place [which] they occupy in the sentence, a subject often overlooked by our predecessors, we have been particularly careful; but here again we have frequently been baffled by structural or idiomatical peculiarities of the English language which precluded changes otherwise desirable."

Let us, then, look at some of the pronouns, and see what is the result of the Revisers' having been "*particularly careful.*" We have seen their use of some of the verbs, or rather their misuse of them, and have been much astonished by it; but then, as I have remarked, they were not "*particularly careful*" with respect to them; although the very name "*verb*" ought to have reminded the Revisers that it is the most important part of speech in a sentence, and therefore one about which they should have been "*particularly careful.*"

However, they say that they have been "*particularly careful*" as to the pronouns, so we will turn to them for a little change; as it is more agreeable to contemplate the effects of carefulness than of carelessness, or it ought to be so; but, unfortunately, even this rule is not without its exception, as reference to 1 Cor. vii. 36 will show; for there the insertion of the wrong pronoun actually makes St. Paul seem to sanction the most abominable incest, namely, that a man should marry his own daughter! I do not wonder that one of your correspondents should have exclaimed, " Angels and ministers of grace defend us! What does this mean?"

The passage which has the approval of the Revisers, and concerning the offending word in which, the pronoun, they say they have been "*particularly careful*," is as follows:—
" If any man thinketh that he behaveth himself unseemly toward his virgin *daughter*, if she be past the flower of her age, and if need so requireth, let him do what he will; he sinneth not; let *them* marry." The only persons mentioned in the passage being the father and daughter, to whom else can the pronoun "*them*" refer? But as we cannot

believe that this was St. Paul's meaning, I suggest to the Revisers that, in the really "Revised Version" which is to be published hereafter, the pronoun "*them*" be changed to "*her*"—"let *her* marry." This would get over the difficulty, and, at the same time, would accurately express the meaning of the original; for, as a girl cannot marry herself, the words "let *her* marry" would, of course, mean "let *them* marry," whoever the man might be. But the word "*daughter*," not being in the Greek, might with advantage be omitted. Clearly, the passage as it now stands is very objectionable. In a foot-note to Eph. iii. 13, the Revisers give an optional reading of "*is*" for "*are*," the singular, for the plural of a verb. Why did they not, in a foot-note to 1 Cor. vii. 36, give an optional reading of "*her*" for "*them*," the singular, for the plural of a pronoun?—Yours faithfully,

G. WASHINGTON MOON.

LETTER VI.

Pronouns must agree with their Antecedents. The Revisers "particularly careful" as to Pronouns. Collective Nouns, the rule respecting them.

SIR,—The first rule of grammar respecting pronouns is, that they "must agree with their antecedents." Yet, simple as is this rule, and avowedly careful as the Revisers have been, I fail to see either conformity to the rule or evidence of carefulness in Rev. xx. 13, where we read, "And they were judged *every man* according to *their* works." It should have been, "*Every man* according to *his* works;" unless every man was answerable for the works of all the rest as well as for his own, in which case, but not otherwise, it would have been correct to say that they were judged "*every man* according to *their* works."

In Luke xvi. 15, we read, "Ye are *they* that justify *your*selves." Of course it should be, "*they* that justify *them*selves." See also Acts iii. 26, where, in the Authorised Version, it says correctly, "Turning away every *one* of you from *his* iniquities." But, in the Revised Version, it says, "Turning away every *one* of you from *your* iniquities." And this is called "*Revising* the Scriptures!"

Another instance of the non-agreement of a pronoun with its antecedent is in Matt. vi. 20, 21, "Lay up for *yourselves* treasures in heaven; ... for where *thy* treasure is, there will *thy* heart be also." In the Authorised Version the passage very properly reads thus: "Lay up for *yourselves* treasures in heaven; ... for where *your* treasure is, there will *your* heart be also." If the alteration of the pronoun in this passage is the result of the Revisers' carefulness, it is to be regretted that they were not careless enough to leave the passage as it stood; for they have spoilt the grammar of it, and have given us no additional idea, except that of their own incapacity for putting into good English the treasures of truth contained in the Sacred Scriptures.

What could the Revisers mean by saying that they had been "*particularly careful*" as to the pronouns? It puzzles me. I have said that I fail to find evidence of carefulness; I fail also to find evidence of consistency; for, in the parallel passage in Luke xii. 34, the pronouns are correct; but why in Matthew we read of treasures "*in heaven*," and in Luke of a treasure in "*the heavens*," I have yet to inquire.

In Matt. ix. 6, and in Luke v. 24, we read of "*Thy* house;" but in Luke vii. 44, and in John ii. 17, it is "*Thine* house." Are we to aspirate the "*h*" in the former passage and not in the latter? It seems so; and if so, might it not have been better had they written "*'ouse?*"

In Matt. vii. 24, it is "Every one *which* heareth;" but in the next verse but one it is "Every one *that* heareth." Why this change? So in Col. iv. 11, 12, it is "Jesus *which* is," and "Epaphras *who* is." So also in Luke vi. 48, 49, we read of "A man *who* digged," and "A man *that* built."

Lastly, why is John the Baptist's corpse spoken of as masculine in one passage and as neuter in another? In Matt. xiv. 12, we read, "They took up the corpse, and buried *him;*" but in Mark vi. 29, it says, "They took up his corpse, and laid *it* in a tomb." This inconsistency is not found in the Authorised Version; but then the compilers of that version probably were not "*particularly careful*" as to the pronouns.

The second rule respecting pronouns is as follows:—"When the antecedent is a collective noun conveying the idea of *plurality*, the pronoun must agree with it in the *plural* number; but when the collective noun conveys the idea of *unity*, the pronoun must agree with it in the *singular* number." In Matt. xv. 8, and in Mark vii. 6, we read, "This people honour*eth* me with *their* lips." This sentence is in direct violation of the rule; for here the collective noun "*people*" is evidently singular, as is shown by the verb "honour*eth*." Why, then, have the Revisers made the pronoun which follows the verb plural? They should have altered either the pronoun or the verb.

So also in Acts vii. 34, where it says, " I have surely seen the affliction of my people which *is* in Egypt, and have heard *their* groaning, and I am come down to deliver *them;* " either the pronoun or the verb should have been altered. The *pro-noun* must agree with the *noun for* which it stands. In each of the foregoing passages the verb would be the preferable word to alter.

Again, in John xi. 42, we read, " Because of the multitude which stand*eth* around I said it, that *they* may believe." Here the collective noun "*multitude*" is evidently plural; the pronoun is therefore correctly plural; but the verb is wrong; the sentence should be, " Because of the multitude which *stand* around I said it, that *they* may believe." The same error occurs in Mark iv. 1, 2; and in John xii. 17, 18.

Errors in connection with collective nouns are found also in Mark i. 33, and Acts xiii. 44, where the word "*city*" evidently means the inhabitants individually, and yet the verb is in the singular; *e.g.*, "*All* the city *was* gathered together at the door." In Luke i. 10, it says, "*The whole multitude* of the people *were;*" but in Mark xi. 18, it says, "*All the multitude was* astonished at his teaching." That is just what I am at the English teaching of the Revisers, for, in Col. i. 27, and ii. 3, they write of "*riches*" which "*is*," and of "*treasures*" which "*are;*" and, in John vii. 49, we read, "This multitude which know*eth* not the law *are* accursed." I certainly am not *blessed with a knowledge of the law* which has guided the Revisers in their choice of English. —Yours faithfully,

G. WASHINGTON MOON.

LETTER VII.

English Idiom to be followed. Grecisms. "A Verb must *agree with its Nominative." Error in the Lord's Prayer.*

SIR,—The opinion expressed by the Rev. W. Sanday, D.D., Principal of Bishop Hatfield's Hall, University of Durham,[*] respecting the system upon which a translation of the Greek of the New Testament should be made into English, and has been made by the Revisers, is at variance with the opinions expressed in the Preface of the work by the Revisers themselves.

Dr. Sanday appears to advocate a literal

[*] Rev. W. Sanday, D.D., late Fellow of Trinity College, Oxford, is Principal of Bishop Hatfeld's Hall, University of Durham, and is distinguished as the author of a "Critical Essay on St. John's Gospel," and is a valuable contributor to Bishop Ellicott's New Testament and Commentary.

rendering of the Greek; and, on the ground of Greek usage, justifies " the construction of a singular verb followed by several substantives," a construction which is entirely contrary to English idiom. The Revisers say (Preface, p. xv.), concerning a difference between Greek and English idiom, "In such instances we have not attempted to violate the idiom of our language by forms of expression which it could not bear." So we see that the Revisers very properly laid down for themselves the rule that, where the idioms of the two languages differ, the idiom of that language into which the translation is made is the one which is to be followed.

In further illustration of this they say, p. xvi., respecting the use of the definite article, " Here again it was necessary to consider the peculiarities of English idiom, as well as the general tenor of each passage. Sometimes we have felt it [to be] enough to prefix the article to the first of a series of words to all of which [better '*all which*'] it is prefixed in the Greek.

... Sometimes, conversely, we have had to tolerate the presence of the definite article in our Version when it is absent from the Greek, and perhaps not even grammatically latent; simply because English idiom would not allow the noun to stand alone."

The Revisers, it will be seen, advocated the use of idiomatic English, even when it involved the necessity of sacrificing the literal agreement of the translation with the Greek original; and the object of these letters of mine also is the maintenance of pure idiomatic English, in opposition to the Grecisms into which the Revisers have occasionally been betrayed by their excessive, but commendable, desire to be faithful.

This evidence of their partial failure—and if they had been exempt from failure they would have been more than human—does not seem to have been observed by Dr. Sanday; and, on behalf of the Revisers, he actually takes upon himself the defence of the very errors which, being violations of the system followed by the Revisers, are, I am sure, regretted by them, and will by them be corrected on a future occasion.

Dr. Sanday is a stranger to me, but I am very happy, in defence of the Queen's English, to do battle with him; especially as I find that he has a literary reputation of no mean character. He has challenged my statements, and I gladly take up the challenge. The chief matter in dispute between us is the invariableness of the rule that "a verb *must* agree with its nominative." I maintain that, although a few instances of the violation of the rule exist in the Bible and elsewhere, those instances do not prove that the rule admits of exceptions. It is easy to find violations of any and every rule.

One violation of this rule which we are considering occurs in the doxology at the end of the Lord's Prayer; and if, by some persons, the violation is tolerated there, it is tolerated simply because the sentence in which it occurs is endeared to us by sacred associations. But no English scholar who has any respect for his reputation as such would contend that it is grammatically correct to say, "Thine *is* the kingdom, *and* the power, *and* the glory," for that is saying, "They *is* thine!"

But the statement which Dr. Sanday makes, that "The construction of a singular verb followed by several substantives is far from [being] untenable in English," does not seem to have reference to the doxology in particular, but to have a general reference to similarly constructed sentences, and especially to those which were criticised by me in previous letters. Now if, upon reconsidering the subject, Dr. Sanday thinks that he can support his statement by proofs, let him adduce them. His readers will, I am sure, be deeply interested in being put in possession of the arguments which have so influenced his mind as to satisfy him that a disagreement between a verb and its nominative "is far from [being] untenable in English."

I also, for myself, have to ask Dr. Sanday

for a plain statement of facts in proof of the truth of his assertion that I have made "sweeping and *utterly groundless* charges." I am prepared to show the ground of every charge which I have made; and I must request Dr. Sanday either to substantiate his charge against me or to retract his words. I hope to see his reply in your next number.—
Yours faithfully,

G. WASHINGTON MOON.

LETTER VIII.

Greek Idiom. The Future Auxiliary "will," *and the Verb* "to will."

SIR,—The apologists for the errors in the English of the Revised New Testament asserted as a fact that it had been the intention of the Revisers so to write English that it should be in accordance with Greek idiom. But the ground of that assertion I cut away from under the apologists, by showing in my last letter that the Revisers themselves distinctly avow in their Preface that they had been actuated by a directly opposite intention.

Therefore, where their practice occasionally diverges from any rule which they had laid down, that divergence must in honesty be attributed to carelessness; for it would be absurd to entertain the idea that they would deliberately and intentionally act in opposition to their own wishes. Yet that is the folly with which the apologists unconsciously charge them. Well might the Revisers say, "Save us from our friends; they excuse our errors in English at the sacrifice of our character for consistency."

But why do not the Revisers themselves either justify their use of the condemned expressions, or else acknowledge their inaccuracy? Is public opinion a matter of indifference to the Revisers? If it is, it ought not to be so; for, the Book which they have altered belongs to the public, and the public have a right to be informed respecting the alleged inaccuracies in it. However, perhaps the Revisers are waiting until the list be complete; so we will proceed with our investigations.

Now, although there are many errors in the Revised New Testament which must be attributed to carelessness, there are others which are the result of a deliberate rejection of the opinion of the highest authorities. I will instance one of those errors, one which I know was the subject of discussion among the Revisers, and the avoidance of which was ably advocated by one of the finest English scholars on the Episcopal bench, but he was outvoted and the error remains.

I refer to the confounding of the second person singular of the present tense of the verb "to will" with the second person singular of the future auxiliary "will." Every schoolboy who knows anything of English verbs knows that these are wholly different from each other. The verb "to will" becomes "willest" in the second person singular, while the auxiliary "will" becomes "wilt." Why, then, have the Revisers violated this very simple rule? What has been gained by their doing so? Nothing, except discredit to themselves and pain to every scholar who desires that the Best of Books shall be as free from errors of language as it is free from errors of doctrine.

THE REVISERS' ENGLISH. 41

"Wilt" is used correctly in the Authorised Version in John v. 6, "*Wilt* thou be made whole?" There it is the auxiliary to the passive verb "to be made." Again, in Acts i. 6, we read, "*Wilt* thou at this time restore again the kingdom to Israel?" There also it is proper, because it is the auxiliary to the active verb "to restore." But, in the Revised Version, in Matt. xiii. 28, "*Wilt* thou that we go and gather them up?" it is not the auxiliary to any verb, but is the second person singular of the present tense of the verb "to will," and should therefore be "willest," the meaning being, "*Is it thy will* that we go and gather them up?"

The absurdity of confounding these two words will be apparent when it is considered that the active verb "to will" is expressive of the *present*, whereas the auxiliary "will" is expressive of the *future*. In Mark x. 51 and Luke xviii. 41, we read, "What *wilt* thou that I should do unto thee?" It should be,

"What *willest* thou?" *i.e.*, "What *is* thy *will?*" The error occurs also in Matt. xv. 28, xvii. 4, xxvi. 17, 39; Mark xiv. 12, 36; and Luke ix. 54.—Yours faithfully,

G. WASHINGTON MOON.

LETTER IX.

"Shall" *and* "Will," *the rule for their proper use. The rule respecting Verbs referring to immutable circumstances.*

SIR,—Let us now consider the confounding of the auxiliaries "shall" and "will" in the Revised New Testament, the instances of which are astonishingly numerous. Yet the rule for the proper use of them also is very simple; it is as follows: "If the speaker is the nominative to the verb, and also determines its accomplishment, or if he is neither the nominative to the verb nor determines its accomplishment, the proper auxiliary is 'will,' in every other case it is 'shall.'" See Dr. Ward's "Essays on the English Language," a work quoted with approval by Bishop Lowth.

One or two examples of the error will suffice. In Matt. xxvi. 21, we read, " Verily I say unto you, that one of you *shall* betray me ; " and in verse 34, " Before the cock crow, thou *shalt* deny me thrice."

If we test these sentences by the rule, we shall find that in each case the wrong auxiliary has been used. The speaker was not the nominative to the verb, nor (unless we make Christ the author of evil) did He in either case determine its accomplishment; therefore the proper auxiliary is " will " in the first sentence, and " wilt " in the last.

On the other hand, in Matt. xxiv. 13, we read, " He that endureth to the end, the same *shall* be saved." Here also the speaker is not the nominative to the verb, but he does determine its accomplishment; therefore the auxiliary " shall," which has been used, is the proper one.

The application of this rule, in testing the correctness of the use of either of these auxiliaries, will show how very numerous are the errors which the Revisers have sanctioned in this matter only.

Another rule which the Revisers have violated is this, "Where a speaker or a writer in referring to the past relates a circumstance which is immutable, or supposed to be so, the present tense, and not the past, is to be used." That the Revisers knew this rule is evident from their having corrected a violation of it in the Authorised Version in Heb. xi. 19, where we read, " By faith Abraham offered up Isaac, . . . accounting that God *was* able to raise him up." In the Revised Version that has been altered to " accounting that God *is* able to raise him up."

Yet, in Acts xviii. 28, the Revisers have written, " Apollos powerfully confuted the Jews, and that publicly, showing by the Scriptures that Jesus *was* the Christ." It should be " showing by the Scriptures that Jesus *is* the Christ."

Once more, why have the Revisers said, in Acts ix. 20, that St. Paul " proclaimed Jesus, that he *is* the Son of God;" and in Acts xviii. 5, that St. Paul testified "that Jesus *was* the Christ"?

While writing of the verb "to be," I may as well ask the Revisers why they have said, in Rev. xiii. 10, "Here *is* the patience *and* the faith of the saints"? Are patience and faith one? If they are, then the verb is correct in the singular. But we are told, in Jas. i. 3, that patience is the effect of faith; that being so, if the two are one, then the effect is its own cause!—Yours faithfully,

G. WASHINGTON MOON.

LETTER X.

Dr. Sanday on "a Verb's agreement with its Nominative." Examples of departure from rule leave the rule unchanged.

SIR,—Dr. Sanday says that I challenged him " to produce examples in English of a singular verb in agreement with more than one substantive." If he will refer to my letter, he will see that my challenge was not for him " *to produce examples* " of the errors, for I admitted their existence, and stated that they " do not prove that the rule [respecting a verb's agreement with its nominative] admits of exceptions." My challenge was for Dr. Sanday " to support his statement by *proofs* " that a verb's disagreement with its nominative " is far from being untenable in English." He has not done it, nor did I think that he could; but he has attempted to do it by adducing the three following examples of the error, and assigning some astounding reasons for their existence.

The first example is "father and mother," which, he says, may be considered as "father-and-mother," and be spoken of in connection with a singular verb; I suppose he means because they were married, and so became "no more.twain, but one flesh;" and therefore we ought to say, "Father and mother *was* there!" But the argument is weak; for, either they are two, or they are one: if they are two, the verb is wrong; if they are one, it is not an example of "a singular verb in agreement with *more than one* substantive."

The second example which Dr. Sanday gives is, "Of whom *is* Hymenæus and Philetus;" and of this he says that "the second substantive is added as a kind of afterthought." What *does* Dr. Sanday mean? "Holy men of God spake as they were moved by the Holy

Spirit" (2 Pet. i. 21). Are we, then, to believe that the words " *and Philetus* " were an "*afterthought*" of the Holy Spirit? This is dreadful! And yet, if they really were an "*afterthought*," as Dr. Sanday tells us, they were an afterthought of either the Holy Spirit or of St. Paul; and if the "*afterthought*" did not emanate from the Holy Spirit, it is not inspired. Let Dr. Sanday avoid which horn of the dilemma he pleases, he will be impaled on the other.

The third example which he gives is, " My flesh and my heart fail*eth*;" and this, he says, is to be read thus, " My flesh [faileth] and my heart faileth;" for " The verb in the one clause is intended to be mentally repeated or understood in the other." I should be sorry to think that Dr. Sanday ever sanctions anything approaching to mental reservation, either in speech or in writing. In speech, it is apt to conceal the truth; and, in writing, it would lead to the sanctioning of every conceivable error; for, if ellipses like that are to be allowable, errors of every sort could be explained away, and *right* and *wrong*, with regard to language, would become obsolete terms.

Dr. Sanday quotes similar errors from Shakespeare, and seems to hold the opinion that, because a certain form of speech has occasionally been used by a great writer, it must be correct. But, with respect to examples of departure from rule, I quite agree with the Rev. Matthew Harrison that, "it signifies nothing that this or that expression has been used by Johnson, or Addison, or Swift, or Pope, or any other writer whatever. All those whose names I have mentioned, and innumerable others, have written incorrectly, and their authority will go just as far as it can be supported by grammatical principle, and no farther.

It is not a question of *genius*, but simply a question of *syntax;* and as authors of the highest reputation in English literature are, over and over again, inconsistent with themselves, it is impossible that they can in all cases be right." "Too many persons are satisfied if they can but find a certain phrase in print; they are *more* than satisfied—they are *triumphant*—if they can appeal to an author of reputation. Such a practice must ever have a tendency to perpetuate error. That which is right is right, without any authority at all, and that which is wrong cannot be made right by any authority." (See "The Rise of the English Language," pp. 280, 113, by the Rev. Matthew Harrison, A.M., late Fellow of Queen's College, Oxford.)

Dr. Sanday might have given a stronger reason for the verb being in the singular in the last of the instances which he adduced— "My flesh and my heart faileth." He might have said that the expression "*flesh and heart*" in this passage is equivalent to "*flesh and blood*" in Matt. xvi. 17, and means simply "*the mortal part of man.*" But although it may not be incorrect to say, "Flesh and blood *hath* not revealed it unto thee," the meaning being, "*No one* of flesh and blood *hath* revealed it unto thee," still it is better to avoid the use of expressions which appear to be ungrammatical, and to state unequivocally what we mean.—Yours faithfully,

G. WASHINGTON MOON.

LETTER XI.

The Essentials of a Good Translation. Ambiguity in the Original. The Charge of Carelessness. Errors in the use of Pronouns.

SIR,—With reference to examples in the Greek of the New Testament, I stated in my first letter that my criticisms would be based upon the principle that "two things are essential to a good translation; the one, that it be a *faithful expression* of the ideas intended to be conveyed in the original; and the other, that it be a *grammatical expression* of those ideas according to the idiom of the language into which the translation is made."

To this principle I have constantly adhered, and shall adhere; and in accordance with it, I maintain that the errors in English which I have pointed out cannot be justified by the existence of anything analogous in the Greek.

Of course where the meaning of the Greek is doubtful, the translation must be doubtful. For instance, in Mark i. 9, 10, we read, "It came to pass in those days, that Jesus came from Nazareth of Galilee, and was baptized of John in the Jordan. And straightway coming up out of the water, *he* saw the heavens rent asunder, and the Spirit as a dove descending upon him." It says, "*He* saw." Who saw? Jesus or John? The Greek text is ambiguous, for the verb εἶδε will apply either to Jesus or to John; and the Revisers have, very properly, left the ambiguity. But where there is no ambiguity in the original, the language of the translation should be severely perspicuous.

It is idle to attack my criticisms, for they are based upon the principle which I quoted. If the principle is wrong, let the apologists show its fallaciousness—let them destroy the foundation, and the superstructure will fall of itself. As to the charge of "*carelessness*" which I brought against the Revisers, if the apologists object to it let them substitute for it "*careful-*

ness" if they like; but, in a translation, "*carefulness*" respecting the original is no sufficient apology for "*carelessness*" respecting the laws of the language into which the translation is made.

The Revisers have been "*particularly careful*" or "*careless*" as to the pronouns, hence the following inconsistencies. In Matt. xxiv. 2, we read, " There shall not be left here one stone upon another, *that* shall not be thrown down;" but, in the parallel passage in Mark xiii. 2, we read, "There shall not be left here one stone upon another, *which* shall not be thrown down." This inconsistency is not found in the two passages in the Authorised Version. Why have the Revisers varied the relative pronouns in the Revised Version? Is it consistent with the rule of "introducing as few changes as faithfulness would allow"? (See Preface, p. xv.) Or is it consistent with the following passage in p. xiv. of the Preface? —"Where, as in the case of the first three Evangelists, precisely the same clauses or sentences are found in more than one of the

Gospels, it is no less necessary to translate them in every place in the same way." Let me ask also what peculiar difference there was in Christ, Abraham, and Moses, that necessitated a different relative pronoun in speaking of each. We read of "The man *that* is called Jesus," "Abraham *which* is dead," and "Moses *who* put a veil upon his face." See John ix. 11; viii. 53; and 2 Cor. iii. 13. Compare also Matt. x. 4, with Mark iii. 19, "Judas Iscariot, *who* also betrayed Him;" and, "Judas Iscariot, *which* also betrayed Him." The "*particular carefulness*" shown in the Revisers' use of pronouns is certainly very puzzling. In John xvii. 9 and 11 there is a strange alteration: verse 9 in the Authorised Version reads, "*Them which* thou hast given me;" and verse 11 reads, "*Those whom* thou hast given me." But, in the Revised Version, it is verse 9 which reads, "*Those whom;*" and verse 11, "*Them which;*" while verse 20 reads, "*Them that.*"—Yours faithfully,

G. WASHINGTON MOON.

LETTER XII.

"*Three Alternatives.*"   *Anonymous Correspondence.
The Auxiliary* "will."   "Shall" *once the only
Future Auxiliary.   The Verb* "to will."

SIR,—One of the apologists, who signs himself " A Former Fellow and Tutor of ——— College, Oxford," having kindly volunteered to enlighten me upon the fact that many of the violations of English grammar which I have exposed "are really faithful renderings of the Greek," I have much pleasure in returning the kindness by recommending to him a course of study in " English words derived from the Latin," as I notice that he uses the expression " *three alternatives !* "

Is it not a pity that he does not sign his name to his letters? The prestige of it might add weight to his arguments, and invest his statements with authority. However, he probably has good reasons for concealing his name, and we must good-humouredly leave them unchallenged; for, the result of his encounters will, I do not doubt, show that he has acted wisely. Doubtless, as a former Fellow and Tutor of one of the colleges at Oxford, he is very learned in all that is taught there; but, as English is not included in the curriculum, a little ignorance on that subject must not be severely criticised. I will, therefore, deal gently with him.

His last letter is on the auxiliary verb "*will*," and he gravely assures us that "*wilt*" in the Authorised Version of John v. 6, "*Wilt* thou be made whole?" which I had said was the auxiliary to the passive verb "to be made" is "nothing of the sort!" I suppose he thinks that "*will*" as an auxiliary is expressive of futurity only, and he is unaware of the fact that the auxiliaries were originally regular verbs, and that, as auxiliaries, they still retain somewhat of their original meaning.

For instance, "*shall*," which in very old English is the only future auxiliary, is the Saxon *scealan*, to *owe*, and is used with that signification by Chaucer, who says, in his "Court of Love," "For by the faithe I *shall* to God," *i.e.*, "For by the faith I *owe* to God;" and the word "*shall*" still expresses obligation but is simply an auxiliary; whereas "*will*," which is the Saxon *willan*, and expresses willingness, still exists as a regular verb, *e.g.*, "To will is present with me" (Rom. vii. 18); and this meaning of the regular verb is found, in many instances, in the auxiliary, and notably in the passage under consideration, "*Wilt* thou be made whole?" *i.e.*, "*Art thou willing* to be made whole?" or, as the Revisers have rendered it, "*Wouldest* thou be made whole?" "*would*" being the conditional form of "*will*," and equally with it expressive of volition, but with this difference in the foregoing sentences: "*Wouldest* thou be made whole?" means "Wouldest thou ... if it *were* possible?" But, "*Wilt* thou be made whole?" means, "Wilt thou ... seeing that it *is* possible?" The inclination of the will is expressed, if absolute, by the particle "*will;*" if conditional, by the particle "*would.*" (See Bishop Lowth's "Grammar," page 55, Edition 1804; see also Harris's "Hermes," Book I., chapter viii.)

The auxiliary "*will*" has two meanings: the one expressive of volition, as I have shown, the other expressive of futurity; and it is remarkable that when it is used with the second person, in an interrogative sentence, it is expressive of the former; and when it is used with the very same words inverted so as to form an affirmative sentence, it is expressive of the latter, *e.g.*, "*Will* you go tomorrow?" is an inquiry respecting volition; but "You *will* go to-morrow" is an affirmation of a future event, and does not necessarily imply any volition in either the person spoken to or the person speaking; indeed, the event may be in direct opposition to the will of both.—Yours faithfully,

G. WASHINGTON MOON.

LETTER XIII.

Anonymous Correspondence, " A Country Scholar."
A Verb's agreement with its Nominative. A
Misogynist.

SIR,—There is a great disadvantage inseparable from publishing detached criticisms in a series of letters in a periodical rather than in a volume. The reading of them is unavoidably spread over a long time; and I can clearly see, by the replies to some of my letters, that the writers have either not read the whole of what I have written upon the subject, or they have, through lapse of time, forgotten important statements which I made respecting the basis of my criticisms. Hence, what I much regret, the necessity for repetition in my letters, or else the appearing to leave unanswered certain remarks which, to some persons, may seem like weighty objections newly raised; when, in fact, they are but repetitions of objections to which I have already replied.

Of this class are the objections raised by one who signs himself "A Country Scholar." By the by, why do all my critics, with the very honourable exceptions of Dr. Sanday and the Rev. A. Plummer, write against me anonymously? Doubtless they consider it safest to do so; and probably the idea of personal safety greatly influences such warriors as fire on an enemy from behind a "college" wall or a "country" hedge; but such warfare does not come up to an Englishman's notion of being "valiant in fight" (Heb. xi. 34). Certainly I shall not follow their example, but shall continue to sign my name to every statement which I make, and be prepared either to defend the position which I take up, or, on the evidence of truth, to acknowledge that the position is indefensible, and fearlessly retire from it.

"A Country Scholar" speaks of a verb's

agreement with its nominative as being " Mr. Washington Moon's rule!" It is no more my rule than the English language is mine. The language belongs to us all, and the rule belongs to the language. He further says, " In Acts xvii. 34, Mr. Moon's subservience to his rule, that a multitude of nominatives demands a verb in the plural, puts him into a curious plight. If our Revisers" [the writer does not mean " *our* Revisers," but the New Testament Revisers] " had used the plural (and there is no verb at all in their text), then Damaris, a woman, would have been enumerated among men, ἄνδρες, which would have been more curious English than even that which offends Mr. Moon, which, in fact, is not curious English at all, but natural and good." I can only reply that if, to my critic, " it is not curious English at all, but natural and good," to say, " Among whom *was* Dionysius the Areopagite, *and* a woman named Damaris, *and* others with them," he must indeed be " A *Country Scholar.*"

It is true that in the Greek text there is no verb expressed in the latter clause of the passage; but, unquestionably, a verb is understood; for, without one, the passage would convey no meaning whatever; and it was for that very reason that the Revisers inserted the word "was," which I maintain ought to have been "were," because the verb refers to others besides Dionysius; and the nominative being plural, the verb also should have been plural. The passage is as follows: "Thus Paul went out from among them. But certain men clave unto him, and believed: among whom also was [*were*] Dionysius the Areopagite, and a woman named Damaris, and others with them." If the verb in the latter clause refers to Dionysius only, what is the meaning of the after part of the sentence, "and a woman named Damaris, and others with them"?

I shall be glad if "A Country Scholar" will answer this question, and at the same time tell me wherein consists the *curiousness* of a woman being "*among*" men. St. Luke was not writing of a monastic institution; and the experience of "A Country Scholar" must be strangely different from that of most persons if to him the fact of a woman being "*among*" men is "*curious.*" Perhaps he is a misogynist.—Yours faithfully,

G. WASHINGTON MOON.

LETTER XIV.

The Subjunctive Mood of Verbs. "If it be" and "If it is." "Though he were" and "Though he was." "The Indicative Past."

Sir,—Let us now consider the subjunctive mood of verbs. There are few subjects connected with the grammar of our language which are so imperfectly understood by would-be grammarians as are the rules governing the subjunctive and indicative moods when the verb is preceded by such conjunctions as *if, though, whether, unless,* &c. Hence the ridiculous criticisms which we sometimes see on this subject. Evidently the writers think that the verb following those conjunctions must always be in the subjunctive mood.

One of such critics recently took upon himself to condemn the Revisers of the New

Testament for having, in Rom. iv. 2, altered the Authorised Version, and written "If Abraham *was* justified by works," and to commend them for having written, in Matt. xxvi. 39, "If it *be* possible, let this cup pass away from me;" whereas the former sentence, which he condemns, is grammatically correct; and the latter, which he commends, is absolutely wrong; for, our Saviour was not praying for future deliverance, but for present. Had he been praying for future deliverance, the expression "If it *be* possible" would have been correct; for, it implies a future contingency, and means, "If it [*should*] *be* possible;" but our Saviour's meaning was, "If it [*now*] *is* possible, let this cup pass away from me." And just as our Saviour's prayer did not refer to the future, so neither did St. Paul's remark, in Rom. iv. 2, respecting Abraham; hence the necessity for the verb in each instance to be in the indicative mood; for, "the subjunctive mood, in English, is not used with propriety when we speak of that which is past or that which is present, but, when the fact itself has not yet taken place, and is necessarily future." See Harrison's "English Language," pp. 286, 287; Gould Brown's "Grammar of English Grammars," 2nd Edition, p. 577, Note ix.; and Lindley Murray's 8vo "English Grammar," vol. i. p. 307.

He who would condemn the Revisers for having written, "If Abraham *was* justified by works, he hath whereof to glory," would, doubtless, condemn them also for having changed the passage, in Heb. v. 8, in the Authorised Version, from " though he *were* a son, yet learned he obedience by the things which he suffered," to " though he *was* a Son," &c.; but the Revisers were right in doing so, as they were also in writing, in 2 Cor. viii. 9, "though he *was* rich, yet for your sakes he became poor."

The reason why, in these two passages the verb is put in the indicative *past* instead of *present*, as mentioned in my ninth letter, is because it was the writer's object to emphasise the fact of Christ's sonship and riches *at the time of His humiliation.* The reader can test the correctness of these passages by the rules quoted; and if critics would always quote the rules and authorities for their assertions, the value, or haply the worthlessness, of their criticisms would at once be apparent.—Yours faithfully,

G. WASHINGTON MOON.

LETTER XV.

"If," "Though," "Whether," "Unless," &c. *The Subjunctive Mood, the Rule for its Use. Dr. Angus's Rule. The Revisers' Violation of all Rules.*

SIR,—Apart from any quotation of grammatical rules, the incorrectness of the passage, in Rom. iv. 2, in the Authorised Version, " If Abraham *were* justified by works, he hath whereof to glory," admits of easy demonstration by an appeal to common sense. "*If*" is the Saxon *gif*, from *gifan*, to give, and means *given* or *granted*. Now, substitute *given* for its equivalent *if*, and the passage will read thus: " Given Abraham *were* justified by works, he hath whereof to glory;" or, transposing the words, " Abraham *were* justified by works, give [or grant that, then] he hath whereof to glory." But who would say "Abraham *were* justified"? Clearly it should be "Abraham *was* justified."

I shall have something to say hereafter on *if, though, whether, unless,* and such words; but there is more to be said first about the subjunctive mood, the Revisers' use of which is very uncertain. I thought once that I had discovered their system of using it; but the idea had to be abandoned, and I am obliged to confess that I cannot reconcile their practice with any rule whatever. I found that it was not in accordance with the rule which I have quoted, and I thought that perhaps their system was to "use the subjunctive when in a conditional clause it is intended to express doubt or denial." But neither is their practice in accordance with that; for, in John x. 24, 25, we read, "The Jews said . . . If thou *art* the Christ, tell us plainly. Jesus answered them, I told you, and ye believe not."

Here we have it stated, on the highest authority, that the Jews spoke in "doubt or denial;" and yet the verb is in the indicative mood, and properly so according to the rule quoted in my previous letter; but improperly so according to Dr. Angus's "Handbook of the English Tongue," p. 308, whence I have copied the rule last quoted.

Again, in 1 Cor. xv. 16, we read, "If the dead *are not* raised, neither hath Christ been raised." This sentence also is correct according to the rule first quoted, but quite at variance with Dr. Angus's rule; for, surely St. Paul "intended to express doubt or denial" of the *non*-raising of the dead.

So, also, in Luke xxiii. 35, we read, "The rulers also scoffed at him, saying, He saved others; let him save himself, if this *is* the Christ of God." The word "*scoffed*," in this passage, shows that the rulers "intended to express doubt or denial;" therefore, according to Dr. Angus's rule, the verb ought to have been in the subjunctive; but it is in the indicative, and correctly so according to the rule first quoted by me, and given by the ablest grammarians as the rule governing this construction.

But, though the Revisers' practice is generally in accordance with this rule, it is, as I have said, sometimes at variance with all known rules; *e.g.*, in John vii. 16, 17, we read, " Jesus said, My teaching is not mine, but his that sent me. If any man willeth to do his will, he shall know of the teaching whether it *be* of God, or whether I speak from myself." Was there " doubt or denial " there? Certainly not. Was Christ speaking of the future? Yes, with regard to the verb *to know*, but not with regard to the verb *to be*, which is the verb that we are considering.

Once more; in Acts iv. 19, we read, " Peter and John answered and said, Whether it *be* right in the sight of God to hearken unto you rather than unto God, judge ye." Did Peter and John " intend to express doubt or denial"? Certainly not. Were they speaking of the future? Quite the contrary. According to what rule in English, then, have the Revisers put the verb in the subjunctive mood? I do not know: let them tell us.

There are many other instances of this error; but it is not my purpose to give a complete list of all errors of every kind in the Revised New Testament, but to give specimens of the principal errors. It will be time enough to give a complete list when I know that there is to be a revision of the Revision —" a consummation devoutly to be wished."— Yours faithfully,

G. WASHINGTON MOON.

LETTER XVI.

The Rev. John C. Hyatt. A Verb and its Nominative. An "Alternative Dilemma." "Under the Circumstances." An Irish Bull.

SIR,—Another combatant enters the arena to do battle with me, and, as he comes with his visor up, I honour him and give him a cordial welcome, for I like to see my opponent's face and know with whom I am contending. A fearless manly bearing commands even an adversary's respect.

The Rev. John C. Hyatt, M.A., Vicar of Queensbury, takes up the old argument respecting a verb and its nominative, and contends that, because certain writers have occasionally used language containing a verb in the singular with more than one noun as a nominative, it must therefore be grammatically correct to do so.

THE REVISERS' ENGLISH.

Having already, in my tenth letter, answered that argument, I consider it needless to say more upon it. Nor do I see much necessity to notice his statement that some persons say, " There *is* soup, and fish, and beef, and kidneys, and pudding, and cheese " for dinner. The language of cooks and restaurant waiters is not generally accepted as exemplarily correct.

But there is one passage in the Rev. John C. Hyatt's letter which has greatly interested me. He says, " I have no desire to impale another on the dreadful horn of an alternative dilemma, nor have I any wish for that position myself. I think Mr. Moon's contention is, that under no circumstances can a singular verb be used in English in agreement with more than one substantive, except in error."

Will my clerical critic have the kindness to tell me what he means by " an alternative dilemma " ? Reference to the origin of these two words, in the Latin and Greek languages respectively, shows that every " dilemma " is an "alternative ;" what, then, is "an alternative

alternative," beyond being a fine specimen of tautology?

Equally puzzling is my critic's expression, "under no circumstances." Clearly, he did not realise the meaning of the words which he was using; for, "circumstance" (L. *circumstantia—circum* and *sto, stans*) means "a standing around;" it is, therefore, more in accordance with the derivation of the word to say, "*in* no circumstances," than to say, "*under* no circumstances;" and I presume that the former is what he meant. He may, however, console himself that he is not alone in committing this error; the Revisers err in like manner in their Preface, p. xx.

Once more; my critic says, "I think Mr. Moon's contention is, that under [*in*] no circumstances can a singular verb be used in English *in agreement* with more than one substantive, except *in error*." This is as thoroughly Irish as is "under no circumstances;" for if the verb is "in agreement," it is not "in error;" and if it is "in error," it is not "in agreement." What strange infatuation can have seized the Rev. John C. Hyatt that immediately after saying that he had no wish to be impaled "on the dreadful horn of an alternative dilemma" (whatever that is), he actually impales himself on the horns of an "Irish bull!"

As I do not think that he is seriously hurt by the impalement, I cannot but smile and leave him to wriggle off as best he may, while I resume my criticisms on the English of the Revised New Testament.—Yours faithfully,

G. WASHINGTON MOON.

LETTER XVII.

"If," "Though," "Whether," "Unless," &c. *The Derivation of* "If." "If" *used for* "Whether." "Though" *used for* "If." *The Derivation of* "Though."

SIR,—The Revisers are very eccentric in their use of the words "if," "though," "whether," "unless," &c. The little conjunction "if" seems to be used as a kind of "fag" to the big conjunctions "though" and "whether," and made to do duty for both; while "except" and "unless" waltz round and round, occupying each other's positions, in all the delightfully bewildering mazes of a dance, to the singular music of the Revisers' sentences.

Unfortunately the public do not sympathise either with the music or with the dance; and a wailing cry comes to us from the

Revisers, as from "children sitting in the market-place and saying, We have piped unto you, and ye have not danced; we have mourned to you, and ye have not wept" (Luke vii. 32). No doubt we are very ungrateful; but it is because we have not received that which we had a right to expect, namely, that the Best of Books would be translated into the best of language. The conjunction "if," as I mentioned in a former letter, means "give" or "grant;" it, is the imperative of the Saxon "gifan," to give, and has come down to us through the stages "gef," "yef," "yf." The Scotch is "gif," and in some counties "gin," with the hard *g;* the former is "give," and the latter "gi'en," a contraction of "given."

The conjunction "if" is very often improperly made to do duty for "whether" and "though." But "if" requires the word "then" to be either expressed or understood in the sentence in order to complete it; whereas "whether," which means "which of either," is

F

followed by "or" or by "or not" either expressed or implied.

On turning to Mark xv. 44, in the Revised Version, we there find both words, the one used incorrectly, and the other correctly. The passage is as follows: "And Pilate marvelled *if* he were already dead: and calling unto him the centurion, he asked him *whether* he had been any while dead" (or, according to the foot-note, "were already dead"), "and when he learned it of the centurion, he granted the corpse to Joseph."

Here the words "if he were" should be "whether he was:" Pilate marvelled, or wondered, *whether he was dead or not;* and, in order to satisfy himself he asked the centurion. Had there been in Pilate's mind no doubt as to the fact of Christ's death, but only astonishment that He had died so quickly, then the sentence would have been, "Pilate marvelled *that* he was already dead;" but as there was doubt, the proper conjunction is not "if," but "whether."

THE REVISERS' ENGLISH.

Not only do the Revisers make "if" do duty for "whether," but they make it do duty for "though" likewise; and sometimes, by way of compensation I suppose, they make "though" do duty for "if;" and yet how different are the meanings of the two words! "If" implies that there is no opposition, the thing being "granted;" but "though," being equivalent to "notwithstanding that," expressly implies the existence of opposition.

"Though" is the imperative of the Saxon "*thafian*," to allow. "If" and "though" have, therefore, similar origins, and are frequently confounded; but a distinction is preserved between them among accurate writers. Instances of "if" being used for "though" are found in 1 Cor. xiii. 1–3, and of "though" being used for "if," in 1 Cor. vii. 30, and elsewhere; but I select Luke ix. 53, because there the conjunction has no corresponding word in the Greek text, so that the error rests entirely with the Revisers.

The passage reads thus, "And they did not

receive him, because his face was *as though he were* going to Jerusalem." It should be, "*as if he was* going to Jerusalem," because, as I have said, the conjunction "though" implies opposition, but there is no opposition intended to be implied in the passage quoted; quite the contrary, there is apposition, but no opposition. "His face was *as if* he was going to Jerusalem."

The error occurs also in 2 Cor. x. 14; and yet, in verses 2 and 9 of the very same chapter, the correct form is used; thus: "*As if* we walked according to the flesh," and "*As if* I would terrify you by my letters."—Yours faithfully,

G. WASHINGTON MOON.

LETTER XVIII.

"If" *used for* "Though." *The "Edinburgh Review" on the Revised New Testament.*

SIR,—It is very strange that the Revisers, having in nearly a score of passages erroneously used "though" for "if," should, in the first three verses of 1 Cor. xiii., have four times erred in the opposite manner, and used "if" for "though;" thus making wrong what was absolutely right in the Authorised Version, and weakening the whole force of the Apostle's argument.

The passage is the well-known one on "charity," or "love" as the Revisers have chosen to call it. In the Authorised Version it reads thus: "*Though* I speak with the tongues of men and of angels, . . . and *though* I have the gift of prophecy, . . . and *though* I have all faith so that I could remove mountains, . . . and *though* I bestow all my goods to feed the poor, . . . and *though* I give my body to be burned, and have not charity, it profiteth me nothing."

In each of these instances the Revisers have substituted " if " for " though ; " and I think I can divine their reasons for making the change —they wished to show that the Apostle Paul was speaking hypothetically; and they felt that the words "though I speak" are not hypothetical, but directly affirmative. Now, there can be no doubt that St. Paul was stating a hypothetical case, for he never would have affirmed that he himself spoke " with the tongues of men and of angels," for he tells us, in 2 Cor. x. 10, that it was said of his speech that it was " contemptible."

But did it never occur to the Revisers that they might still retain that powerful conjunction " though," and yet, through it, express that hypothesis? Would not the Apostle's meaning be accurately rendered if the translation were as follows:—" *Though I were to* speak with the tongues of men and of angels," &c. ? Of course it will be objected that, in this rendering, the Greek and English verbs do not agree in mood and tense; but do not the words accurately express the Apostle's *meaning?* I honour the Revisers for their conscientious fidelity to the original text; and we must all confess that, as a *literal* translation, their work is of inestimable value, especially as a basis for a future free translation into pure idiomatic English.

As the *Edinburgh Review* says : — " The chief use of the present attempt will be as a work of reference in which the grammatical niceties of the New Testament diction are treated with laboured fidelity. But it will no more furnish an Authorised Version to eighty millions of English-speaking people than any number of *mémoires pour servir* will give them a standard history. It will remain a monument of the industry of its authors and a treasury of their opinions and erudition; but, unless we entirely mistake, *until its Eng-*

lish has undergone thorough revision it will not supplant the Authorised Version." . . . . " Every phase of New Testament scholarship was represented in the New Testament Company, but the niceties of idiomatic English appear to have found no champion." — *Edinburgh Review*, No. 315, pp. 188, 173. I would say, rather, that the champions were outvoted.
—Yours faithfully,

G. WASHINGTON MOON.

LETTER XIX.

"Wilt" *and* "Willest." "Purpose" *and* "Propose." "To go" *and* "To come." "Only" *and* "Alone."

Sir,—Does not the Rev. John C. Hyatt know that, in speaking of verbs, it is customary to speak of them as they are in their infinitive mood form? We do not say, "The verb *go*," but "The verb *to go*;" so likewise we do not say, "The verb *be made*," but "The verb *to be made*." The Rev. John C. Hyatt either does not know this fact, or he does know it. If he does not know it, his acquaintance with grammatical writings must be small indeed; and if he does know it, then he appears to have wilfully perverted the meaning of my words, for in commenting on my statement, that "*wilt*," in the sentence "Wilt thou be made whole?" is the auxiliary to the passive verb "*to be made*," he quotes certain authorities to show that "no *auxiliary* ever admits the preposition *to* after it," as if I had said that it did! (See pp. 41, 58-60.)

The meaning of my statement is obvious enough to any one of ordinary intelligence, and cannot but by wilful perversion be construed to mean anything else than that *in the sentence*, "Wilt thou be made whole?" "*wilt*" is the auxiliary to the verb. Had the translators intended to express the second person singular of the verb "*to will*," they should have said "*willest*" not "*wilt*" (see Bishop Lowth's "Introduction to English Grammar," ed. 1804, p. 44). There is no such word as "*wilt*" in any part of the verb "*to will*," it is purely a form of the auxiliary.

"*Propose*" for "*purpose*" is another word which the Revisers misuse: not, indeed, in the New Testament itself, for there they had the Authorised Version to guide them, but in their Preface, p. xi., where they say, "We now pass onward to give a brief account of the particulars of the present work. This we *propose* to do under the four heads," &c.

To *propose* to do a thing is to offer to do it subject to another's approval; but that was not the Revisers' intention, for they knew that, without giving any one the opportunity of approving or of disapproving, they should proceed to do that which they had *purposed;* and "*purpose*" is the word which they ought to have used, seeing that they had determined upon the course to be taken.

"*Propose*" and "*purpose*" have had the same origin (Latin "*propono*," *to place before*), but they have different meanings. That which I "*propose*" I *place before another* for his approval; that which I "*purpose*" I *place before myself* to be done. Paul *proposed* to Barnabas to visit the brethren in every city wherein they had proclaimed the word of the Lord (Acts xv. 36). Subsequently Paul *purposed* in spirit to go to Jerusalem (Acts xix. 21).

This reminds me of another error. In Rom. i. 13 the Revisers make St. Paul say, in writing to Rome from Corinth, "Oftentimes I purposed *to come* unto you;" but St. Paul did not purpose "*to come*" to the Romans; he was at Corinth and purposed *to go* to them.

In Matt. xiv. 29, also, the same error occurs. There we read, "And Peter went down from the boat, and walked upon the waters *to come* to Jesus." Clearly, he walked upon the waters *to go* to Jesus. In the Authorised Version it is correctly "*to go* to Jesus," and why the Revisers (so-called) have altered it I am at a loss to understand.

Speaking of words which are of similar but not of synonymous import, I remark that the Revisers have fallen into the very common error of using "*alone*" for "*only;*" *e.g.*, in Luke v. 21, they say, "Who can forgive sins but God *alone?*" And in the next chapter, verse 4, they say of the shewbread, "Which it is not lawful to eat save for the priests *alone.*" In each of these cases the idea

THE REVISERS' ENGLISH.

intended to be conveyed is not that of *loneliness*, but that of *oneness*, and therefore the word "*only*" (literally *one-ly*) should have been used.

"*Alone*" means "apart," "distant from others;" but "*only*" means that there are no others. Our Saviour did not mean what the Revisers' words imply; namely, that the law was that the shewbread was to be eaten by *the priests when alone;* His meaning was that *only the priests* might eat it. So also our Saviour did not mean that when *God was alone* He forgave sins; our Saviour's meaning was that *only God* forgave sins. I am surprised that the Revisers have so egregiously erred in stating so plain a truth.—Yours faithfully,

G. WASHINGTON MOON.

LETTER XX.

"Except" *and* "Unless."

SIR,—The Revisers appear to have had no fixed rule for their guidance in the use of the words "*except*" and "*unless;*" hence, as I said in a former letter, they are made to occupy each other's positions with bewildering eccentricity. But "*except*" and "*unless*," like the words "*if*" and "*though*," "*purpose*" and "*propose*," and many other pairs of words which were once similar in meaning and were used interchangeably, have now a separate office assigned to each by all accurate writers and speakers.

The distinction between the words is this: —"*Except*," which is the imperative of the verb "to except," is now ranked among the prepositions, that is, it applies to *substantives;*

whereas "*unless*," which is the imperative of the Saxon "*onlesan*," "to dismiss," applies exclusively to *verbs*; or, avoiding grammatical terms, we may say that "*except*" is used with reference to persons and things, and "*unless*" with reference to actions.

Examples of the correct use of "*except*" are found in Acts viii. 1; there we read, "They were all scattered abroad throughout the regions of Judæa and Samaria, *except the apostles;*" and in Acts xxvi. 29; there we read, "I would that . . . all that hear me this day, might become such as I am, *except these bonds.*"

An example of the correct use of "*unless*" will be found in the Revisers' Preface, p. xxi.; there we read, "Such a work can never be accomplished by organised efforts of scholarship and criticism, *unless assisted* by Divine help." But in the same Preface, p. x., there is, unfortunately, an example of the use of the word "*except*" instead of "*unless*," as follows: "To retain no change in the Text on the second final revision by each Company, *except* two thirds of those present *approve* of the same." It should be "*unless* two thirds . . . *approve* of the same."

The Revisers, you see, are not consistent in their use of the words in their Preface; how, then, can we expect to find them consistent in their use of them in the Revised Version of the New Testament? There are there more than forty instances of this one error. I will select one or two as examples.

In 1 Cor. xiv. 9, in the Authorised Version, we read, "*Except* ye utter by the tongue words easy to be understood, how shall it be known what is spoken?" This the Revisers have very properly altered into " *Unless* ye utter," &c. But in the very next chapter, 1 Cor. xv. 2, they have, with incomprehensible inconsistency, done the very reverse: they have substituted " except " for " unless " where " unless " was correct, and " *except* " is wrong!

The passage in the Authorised Version correctly stands thus, " *Unless* ye have believed in vain." In the Revised Version it is "*Except* ye believed in vain." What can have been the motive which actuated the Revisers to alter "*Unless* ye have believed" into "*Except* ye believed," after having just altered "*Except* ye utter" into "*Unless* ye utter"?

The inconsistency is found likewise in verses 5 and 6 of this same chapter xiv.; there, instead of "*Unless* he interpret," the Revisers have written "*Except* he interpret;" yet in the very next verse they have correctly altered "*Except* I shall speak" into "*Unless* I speak."

But in all these instances, and in all others like them where the word has reference to an action, and not simply to persons or things, the correct word is "*unless*," and not "*except*." The Revisers should not have written, "*Except* ye believe," but "*Unless* ye believe that I am he, ye shall die in your sins" (John viii. 24). The error is very common; but no error, whether common or uncommon, should have a place in the Word of God.—Yours faithfully,

G. WASHINGTON MOON.

LETTER XXI.

Result of being Tossed by an Irish Bull. Insipient and Incipient. Blasphemy. Less *and* Fewer. *Derivation of* "Circumstances," Wilt *and* Willest, Subterfuge.

SIR,—In my letter respecting the Rev. John C. Hyatt's misadventure with the Irish bull, I expressed a belief, embodying a hope, that he was not seriously hurt; but evidently he is very much shaken; and he is so angry with me for laughing at him that he incoherently charges me with using "Words of reproach, from insipient silliness down to blasphemy."

I am truly sorry to see that the concussion has somewhat affected the reverend gentleman's mental vision, so that at present he is a little confused as to the position of some of the boundaries of truth and error; but probably, when he has recovered from the sad effects of his fall, he will be able to think more calmly, and then will understand that "incipient," [meaning "*the beginning of*," which, I suppose, is what he meant, should be spelt with a "*c*," and not with an "*s*" as he has spelt it; and that "blasphemy" is rather too strong a word to apply even to the awful sin of jesting about a clergyman's errors in English.

You see that I give him credit for meaning "incipient;" for, to suppose that he really meant "insipient," would be to suppose him again guilty of tautology, the meaning of "insipient silliness" being "silly silliness!"

In a previous letter I said that there are disadvantages in publishing detached criticisms in a periodical; but there are advantages also, one of which is that the criticisms call forth counter-criticisms, which show either where you are in error, or where your language has not been sufficiently explicit to make your meaning clearly understood.

Another advantage is, that your critic is sure to be caught tripping in the very words which he employs to criticise yours, for there probably is not one in ten thousand educated Englishmen who thoroughly knows his own language.

Therefore each writer furnishes additional errors for correction, as does the Rev. John C. Hyatt, who falls into the very obvious and frequently exposed error of using the word "*less*," which is an adjective referring to *quantity in bulk*, for the word "*fewer*," which is an adjective referring to *quantity in number*. He speaks of the phrase, " under the circumstances," as being used " no *less* than four times." He should have said " no *fewer* than four times."

As the Rev. John C. Hyatt characterises as " ridiculous " my saying that the word " circumstance " comes from the Latin word " *circumstantia*," I challenge him to show his superior wisdom by informing your readers as to what *he* considers to be the derivation of the word.

In the meantime, [by way of assisting his studies,] I refer him to "The Critical Latin-English Lexicon, founded on the larger Latin-German Lexicon of Dr. Wm. Freund, with additions and corrections from the Lexicons of Gesner, Facciolati, Scheller, Georges, &c., by E. A. Andrews, LL.D.;" also to Riddle's "English-Latin Lexicon," where he will find " Circumstance, *circumstantia,* Quintilian;" and if the reverend gentleman, who gives us to understand that he studied Latin at Oxford, wants other authorities on the subject I will furnish him with them.

The same reverend gentleman says, "Mr. Moon complains that in my letter I have written '*be made,*' and not '*to be made.*'" The reverend gentleman goes on to say, " I cannot easily believe that the fault he speaks of is due to any error of the printer, because in my copy of the same date the words stand quite correctly as I wrote them, '*to be made.*'"

The reader will see, on referring to my letter (p. 89), that I made no such complaint whatever: my meaning has been strangely misunderstood by my clerical critic.

I should not have taken any notice of his silly remark but for the sweet charity of the sentence which follows it; he says, "Let us hope that this is not a mere subterfuge on the part of one who has nothing else to say." "*Subterfuge*," eh? The reverend gentleman little knows me, if he thinks that I am one to have recourse to "subterfuge!" and as for my having "nothing else to say," I have this to say, that I will not follow his example, and, under the sanctimonious guise of a pious hope, insinuate that *he* has had recourse to subterfuge, but request him to re-read my letter, when he will perhaps be able to comprehend the common sense of my remarks respecting the verb "*to will*," and also see the unwarrantableness of his assertion that, according to my recommendation, we should have to say, "Willest thou to have this woman to thy wedded wife?" Answer: "I will to have." The Rev. John C. Hyatt is certainly one of the densest pupils that I ever tried to instruct; and, had I known the difficulty of getting an idea into his head, I would not have wasted my time in the apparently hopeless task. " *Wilt* thou *have* this woman" is certainly correct, "*wilt*" being the auxiliary to the verb.—Yours faithfully,

G. WASHINGTON MOON.

LETTER XXII.

Tautology. "For ever and ever." "Alway" *and* "Always."

SIR,—There are few errors of language which it is more easy to avoid than those of tautology. A writer may be unfamiliar with the ordinary rules of syntax, and therefore be unconscious of many of the solecisms which are in his sentences; but there cannot be verbal repetitions there and he be ignorant of them.

That being so, and the Revisers having stated in their Preface (p. xiv.) that they had avoided tautology, I am the more surprised to find in their work such passages as the following:—"*From him* that hath not, even that which he hath shall be taken away *from him*" (Luke xix. 26). What do the Revisers mean by "taken away *from him from him*"?

Again, "Thou hypocrite, cast *out* first the beam *out* of thine own eye; and then shalt thou see clearly to cast *out* the mote *out* of thy brother's eye" (Matt. vii. 5). What is meant by casting a beam or a mote "*out out* of the eye"? The repetition does not add to the perspicuity of the sentence, nor would it if multiplied a thousandfold. Indeed, the repetition weakens the force of the sentence, for it leads to the inference that if a second "*out*" is needful, the first "*out*" does not express the idea which is usually conveyed by that word; and, if one "*out*" fails to express it, how can two, or even two thousand, express it?

The same remarks apply to the expression, "*For ever and ever*," which occurs more than a dozen times in the New Testament. If "*for ever*" means "*eternally*," then the words "*and ever*," which follow, are meaningless; for there can be but one eternity stretching from the infinite past to the infinite future; where then is there room for another "*ever*"?

But the words "*and ever*" in the sentence really convey the idea that "*for ever*" does *not* mean "*eternally,*" an idea which the Revisers, I think, did not intend to inculcate; and therefore it is to be regretted that, instead of employing, as they have done, words which have a tendency to destroy the meaning of so vitally important an expression as "*for ever,*" they did not give the literal meaning of the Greek, viz., "*unto ages of ages.*"

While speaking on this subject, I should like to ask the Revisers why they sometimes use the word "*alway,*" and sometimes the word "*always;*" and what difference of meaning they attach to each? For instance, in 2 Thess. i. 3, I read, "We are bound to give thanks to God *alway* for you;" but in verse 11 of the same chapter it is, "We also pray *always* for you." Why is it "*give thanks alway,*" and "*pray always*"? What is there different in the actions that necessitates a difference in the adverbs qualifying those actions? But even in this simple matter the Revisers are not consistent; for, in Acts x. 2, they say, "He was a devout man, and one that . . . *prayed* to God *alway*."

With regard to "backward" and "backwards," "forward" and "forwards," "outward" and "outwards," "upward" and "upwards," the former of each pair of words is the adjective, and the latter is the adverb; but that is not the case with "alway" and "always;" and I shall be glad to know why, in 2 Thess. i. 11, the Revisers say "*pray always*," and in Acts x. 2 say "prayed *alway*."—Yours faithfully,

G. WASHINGTON MOON.

LETTER XXIII.

"Chiefest." *Tautology.* "Footstool of his Feet." "Agreed together." "That, that that." *Tautophany.* "Son" *and* "Sun." "Sleep" *and* "the rest." "Stolen" *and* "Stole away."

SIR,—The desire of the Revisers to be faithful to the Greek original has led them to use some expressions which cannot be described otherwise than as extravagant. For example, they use the word "*chiefest.*" Now, however much as we may sympathise with the Apostle Paul in his humility before God, which prompted him to employ the hyperbolical expression by which he describes himself as being "less than the least of all saints" (Eph. iii. 8), we cannot feel equal sympathy with his boastful expression before men, relative to his position in the Church, when he speaks of himself as being "not a whit behind the *very chiefest* apostles" (2 Cor. xi. 5).

The expression "*chiefest*" cannot be defended on any ground. It implies that the chief is not chief, for it tacitly conveys the idea that there is a "*chiefer*" as well as a "*chiefest;*" both which must be more than "*chief;*" and therefore, as I said, the chief is not chief, which is absurd.

The Revisers have altered Mark x. 44, from "Whosoever of you will be the *chiefest*," to "Whosoever would be *first* among you;" why, then, did they not alter "*chiefest*" to "*chief*," in 2 Cor. xi. 5 and xii. 11, and so make the expression agree with the Apostle's language in 1 Tim. i. 15, "Christ Jesus came into the world to save sinners; of whom I am *chief*"?

Reverting to the subject of tautology, I remark that the Revisers were not satisfied with the word "*footstool*," as given in the Authorised Version, in Matt. v. 35 and elsewhere, but must needs amplify the expression to "*footstool of his feet*," as if the word "*footstool*" could possibly mean a stool for any other part of the body! This is the climax of tautology.

Then, in Acts v. 9, we read, "How is it that ye have *agreed together* to tempt the Spirit of the Lord?" Why "*together*"? How could they *agree* otherwise than *together*? Moreover, if it was needful, in Acts v. 9, to speak of two agreeing "*together*," why was it not needful in Matt. xviii. 19? There it correctly says, "If two of you shall *agree* on earth." What is the difference between "*agreeing together*" and "*agreeing*"?

In Heb. xii. 12, 13, the Revisers say, "Wherefore lift up the hands *that* hang down. . . . *that that* which is lame be not turned out of the way." I wonder that the Revisers, having said, "Wherefore lift up the hands *that* hang down," did not say, "*that that that* is lame be not turned out of the way;" for, according to the rule which I think they have been following, the last "*that*" is as needful as is the first? But how far superior is the English of the Authorised Version! "Wherefore lift up the hands which hang down . . . lest that which is lame be turned out of the way."

In 1 Thess. iv. 15 we read, "This we say unto you by the word of the Lord, *that* we *that* are alive, *that* are left unto the coming of the Lord." In the Authorised Version it is, "that we which are alive, and remain unto the coming of the Lord." It was concerning a similarly excessive use of the word "*that*" that some one said, *that that* "*that*" *that that* man used ought to have been "*which*."

In the same sentence in which the Revisers say that they have avoided tautology, they say that they have avoided "infelicity of sound;" and yet, in Matt. v. 45, they say, "That ye may be *sons* of your Father which is in heaven: for he maketh his *sun* to rise on the evil and the good." In the Authorised version it is, "That ye may be the *children* of your Father which is in heaven;" and so the tautophony, suggestive of a pun, in the Revised Version, was avoided.

A similar fault is found in the Revised Version, in 1 Thess. iv. 13, where we read, "We would not have you ignorant, brethren, concerning them that *fall asleep;* that ye sorrow not, even as *the rest.*" In the Authorised Version it is, "that ye sorrow not, even as *others;*" and so the suggestion of *the rest* taken in sleep was avoided.

This apparent play upon words is very unseemly in the Sacred Scriptures, a remarkable instance of which occurs in Gen. xxxi. 19, 20, where it says, "Rachel had *stolen* the images that were her father's. And Jacob *stole away.*" Doubtless this will be altered in the Revised Version of the Old Testament.—Yours faithfully,

G. WASHINGTON MOON.

LETTER XXIV.

Pronominal Adjectives, "each one ; " "every ; " "*on* either *side*," *for* "*on* each *side ;* " neither, *of ten ; neither,* "nor ; " "both, *of eleven ; *" "*both* of *them ;* " "*both* of *which ;* " "*all* of *them ;* " "*all* of *which.*"

SIR,—It is very strange that, in a work which has been the subject of so much careful thought, there should be errors so numerous and so flagrant as are those in the Revised New Testament.

The Revisers stated that they had been "*particularly careful* as to the pronouns." I suppose that we are to understand that the Revisers' care extended to the pronominal adjectives. Yet, see what has been done with the words, "*each,*" "*either,*" "*neither,*" "*both,*"

H

"*all*," "*naught*," and "*other*" in the Revised New Testament.

First, as to the word "*each*;" in Acts ii. 3, in the Authorised Version, we read, "And there appeared unto them cloven tongues, like as of fire, and it sat upon *each* of them." But in the Revised Version, so called, it is, "and it sat upon *each one* of them." So also, in Rev. iv. 8, in the Authorised Version, we read, "And the four beasts had *each* of them six wings." But, in the Revised Version, it is, "having *each one* of them six wings." Why this alteration? "*Each*" is correct; "*each one*" is incorrect; for, "*each*" means "every *one* of a number separately considered." "*Every*" requires to be followed by the word "*one*," or its equivalent; we cannot say "every knows it;" we must say "every *one*," or "every *person*," &c., knows it. But we can say, "*each* knows it;" which shows that the word "*each*" embodies the word "*one*," and that therefore the word "*one*," in the expression "*each one*," is redundant; and redundancy is a fault; and this particular instance of it occurs more than twenty times in the Revised New Testament.

"*Either*," likewise, is incorrectly used by the Revisers. In John xix. 18, they say, "They crucified him, and with him two others, on *either* side one, and Jesus in the midst." It should be, "on *each* side one;" because "*either*" means one of two, and only the one *or* the other, not both. See Bishop Lowth's "Introduction to English Grammar," p. 115.

As "*either*" means "one of two," so also does its negative "*neither;*" yet the Revisers make it apply to *ten!* See Rom. viii. 38, 39.

The word "*neither*" is correctly followed by "*nor;*" as in the Authorised Version of Luke vii. 33, where it says, "John the Baptist came *neither* eating bread *nor* drinking wine;" but in the Revised Version the passage is *improved* thus:—"John the Baptist is come *eating no* bread *nor* drinking wine." I pass over the inelegancy of the colloquial expression "eating no bread," and simply remark that it is an affirmative assertion, and therefore cannot correctly be followed by "*nor.*" If we must have "eating no bread," then the passage should be, "eating no bread *and* drinking no wine."

The word "*both,*" also, is misused by the Revisers; it means "*the two,*" and cannot correctly be applied to more than two; yet in a foot-note to 1 Cor. i. 30, the Revisers make it apply to three; thus, " Or, *both* righteousness and sanctification and redemption;" and in Acts i. 13, they make it apply to *eleven!*

Another error in the use of the word "*both*" is in the expression "*both of them,*" occurring in Acts xix. 16. "*Of*" is a partitive; but "*both*" means the whole. Therefore it is as absurd to say, "*both of them,*" as it would be to say, "*the whole of the whole;*" for the word "*them*" here means "*both;*" consequently, "*both of them*" is "*both of both.*" It is sufficient to say "*both.*" The word is correctly used in 2 Pet. iii. 1, in the Authorised Version. There we read, "This second epistle, beloved, I now write unto you; *in both which* I stir up your pure minds;" but, in the Revised Version, it is, "*in both of them.*"

For the same reason that we should not say "both *of* them," we should not say "all *of* them," or "all *of* which." We should say "*all*," or "*all which*," as in Col. ii. 22, where, in the Revised Version, we read, "*All which* things are to perish with the using." But why did the Revisers say "*all which*" in Col. ii. 22, and "all *of* which" in their Preface, p. xvi.? The Revisers seem to have had bad memories. Otherwise, in reperusing their work as a whole, these discrepancies would surely have been apparent to them.—Yours faithfully,

G. WASHINGTON MOON.

LETTER XXV.

Tenses of Verbs: "*it* would *appear,*" "*it* would *seem,*" *for* "*it appears*" *and* "*it seems.*" "Aught" *and* "Naught." "Other." "But." *The Logic of Grammar.*

SIR,—The word "*apparent,*" with which I concluded my last letter reminds me of an error in the Revisers' use of the verb "*to appear.*" They have given attention to the Greek aorist, an indefinite *past* tense; but with the *present* and *future* tenses of the verb "*to appear*," they have made strange confusion. It is true that the error is common to other writers, but it is not, on that account, any less an error. When intending to express the *present* tense of the verb, the Revisers have actually used the *future* tense; and instead of saying "*it appears,*" have said "*it would appear.*" See their Preface, p. vi., where we read, "With regard to the Greek Text, *it would appear* that, if to some extent the Translators exercised an independent judgement, it was merely in choosing," &c. It should be, "*it appears* that . . . it was;" not, "*it would appear* that . . . it was;" for that is contingent, and there is no contingency mentioned as affecting the verb "*to appear.*" The error is, as I have said, very common, and it is found in connection with other verbs of a similar meaning; *e.g.,* "*it would seem,*" and "*it would look as if,*" the conditional future being used instead of the unconditional present, "*it seems,*" and "*it looks as if.*"

Reverting to the pronominal adjectives, I remark that the Revisers have made a very unaccountable difference in the spelling of the pronominal adjectives "*aught*" and "*naught.*" The former the Revisers have invariably and correctly spelt "aught;" but the latter, which is the negative form of the same word, they have as uniformly spelt "nought." Had the affirmative form been spelt "*ought*," there would have been some reason in the Revisers' spelling of the negative, though, of course, " two *wrongs* do not make a *right.*" Perhaps this is an instance similar to the one mentioned by my medical friend, whose difficulty and its solution are stated in Letter V., p. 21.

The error of spelling "*aught*" with an "*o*," and thus confusing it with the verb "*ought,*" is very usual, but that it should be spelt with an "*a*" is evident from its derivation: A.-S. *aht*, written also *auht* and *awhit.* Its negative, "*naught*," should certainly agree with it.

With regard to the word "*other*," the Revisers have omitted it where it ought to have been inserted, and have inserted it where it ought to have been omitted. For example, in Mark iv, 31, 32, they tell us that a grain of mustard seed is " less than all the seeds that are upon the earth;" if that is so, then it is less than itself! for, of course, it is one of " all the seeds that are upon the earth." The

Revisers should have said, "less than all *other* seeds." As the passage stands, they state therein, as a fact, an utter impossibility.

In Mark xii. 32, the Revisers insert the word where it should have been omitted; they say of God, "There is none other but he." The word "other" is there redundant; indeed, it is worse than simply redundant, for it distorts the meaning. God is the Self-existent One; and, in that sense, is alone; as He says in Isa. xlv. 18, "I am the Lord, and there is none else." Therefore the passage in Mark xii. 32 should have been, "There is none but he."

The error of using the word "*other*" in this passage which the Revisers have written will be apparent if you consider the meaning of the word "*but*." It is derived from the A.-S. *be-utan*, "to take out," and consequently is equivalent to "*exclude*." Therefore the meaning of the passage is, "If you *exclude* God, there is none other." Admitting the correctness of that statement, then it follows, by a parity of reasoning, that if you *include* God there is *another*. But "*another*" than whom? Clearly another than Himself; so that the passage, as written by the Revisers, affirms, by implication, the existence of at least two Gods!

Dr. Hugh Blair says, in his "Lectures on Rhetoric and Belles Lettres," " There are few sciences in which a deeper and more refined logic is employed than in grammar. It is apt to be slighted by superficial thinkers as belonging to the rudiments of knowledge, which were inculcated upon us in our earliest youth. But what was then inculcated before we could comprehend its principles, would abundantly repay our study in maturer years."

The foregoing remarks, upon the use of the word "*other*," illustrate the Professor's observations.—Yours faithfully,

G. WASHINGTON MOON.

LETTER XXVI.

"To go" *and* "to come." "Come, go!" "Now, then!" *Go* on, *be* off! *Get* off, *get* on. Now *for* then. Good *for* bad. As far as, *and* So far as. *Professor Plumptre. Parentheses. The Name of a Name.*

SIR,—As one of your correspondents has written in defence of the expression contained in St. Paul's Epistle to the Romans, chap i., verse 13, "Oftentimes I purposed *to come* unto you," I revert to the subject, in order to demonstrate, if possible, more clearly why it should be, "Oftentimes I purposed *to go* unto you." Your correspondent admits that, in historic narrative, it would certainly be, "Paul purposed *to go;*" and I add, that as there can be no dispute as to what the apostle purposed to do, namely, "*to go* to

Rome," his language, in writing of his purpose, should undoubtedly be in accordance with it. Your correspondent says of St. Paul, "Why may he not be permitted to use the verb '*to come*,' as *we ourselves* should do in a parallel case?" I do not know whom your correspondent intends to include in his "*we ourselves;*" but I, for one, most emphatically decline the honour. Probably the expression is the journalistic "*we*," and means only the writer himself.

The only occasion on which I can conceive that it would be correct to say, "Oftentimes I purposed *to come* unto you," would be if the speaker were then with those whom he had purposed to visit, and were acquainting them with his previous intention. We speak of *coming* to, or towards, a place *where we are;* and of *going* to a place that is *distant from us.*

The difference between the ancient and the modern use of the words "*go*" and "*come*," in one instance at least, is very remarkable. Formerly, as may be seen in James v. 1, and elsewhere, the expression which, in modern English, is equivalent to "*come*, now," was "*go to*, now." This expression has fallen quite out of use; but we very inconsistently now say to a person whom we wish to send somewhere immediately, "*Come, go!*" and, if he lingers, we perhaps use the equally contradictory expression, "*Now, then!*" following up that by "Go *on!* be *off!*" or "*Get off!* I want you to *get on!*" Truly there are some very strangely contradictory colloquialisms in our language.

While speaking of contradictions, I may as well remark that, in Luke i. 7, the Revisers use the word "*now*," when the meaning is "*then*." Thus, "And they had no child, because that Elizabeth was barren, and they both *were now* well stricken in years." The word "*now*" has no business there, as there is no word corresponding to it in the Greek, and it is not needed to complete the sense; indeed, it is worse than needless; for, the meaning is, "They both *were then* well stricken in years." Besides, the word "*now*" is the more objectionable in that sentence, because the very next sentence begins with "*now*" as an expletive, "*Now*, it came to pass," &c.

Another strange contradiction is the use of the word "*good*" for "*bad*," as in Heb. xi. 12, "There sprang of one, and him as *good* as dead, so many as the stars of heaven in multitude." "*So* many as the stars;" here is another error. "*So—as*," properly refers to a comparison of inequality; "*as—as*," to a comparison of equality; *e.g.*, "There are not *so* many *as* you mention; but there are *as* many *as* we need." The error occurs also in Gal. iv. 1, and Phil. ii. 23. It is found, likewise, in the Revisers' Preface, pp. 8 and 16, where we read, "*So* far *as* can be gathered from the rules," and "*So* far *as* English idiom would allow." In each case it should be "*as* far *as*," not "*so* far *as*," because the statement is affirmative of equality. On page 10 of the Revisers' Preface, the correct form is used; it is as follows—"The principles and rules agreed to by the Committee of Convocation were . . . . To limit, *as* far *as* possible," &c.

Will the Revisers kindly tell me why they used "*as* far *as*" in this sentence, and "*so* far *as*" in the previously quoted sentences? and, especially, why they altered what was correct, in Gal. iv. 1, in the Authorised Version, *viz.*, "The heir, *as* long *as* he is a child," to what is incorrect in the Revised Version, *viz.*, "*So* long *as* the heir is a child"? For rules on this subject, see Booth's "Principles of English Grammar," page 80, and "Handbook of the English Tongue," pp. 320, 321, by Joseph Angus, M.A., D.D., one of the Revisers, who was evidently outvoted on this question, and, doubtless, on many others affecting the English of the Revised New Testament.

Unfortunately, every matter debated by the Revisers was settled, not necessarily according to the judgment of those among them who were best informed upon the subject under discussion, but by the vote of the majority; and we have indubitable evidence that the majority are not good English scholars.

At the recent Church Congress at Newcastle, the Rev. Professor Plumptre, now Dean of Wells, one of the Old Testament Revisers, said, in speaking on this subject, "I venture to think that the names of Ellicott, Lightfoot, Stanley, Trench, Vaughan, Angus, Moulton, carry with them a greater weight of authority in this matter than even that of Mr. Washington Moon."

I will not dispute that point; but, judging from Professor Plumptre's own English in the paper which he read before the Congress, I am compelled to say, that the many errors in his language force upon me the conviction that his opinion as to the correctness of the language of others is but of little value. For example, why does the Professor say, "The names *of* Ellicott, Lightfoot, &c., carry with them a greater weight." The word "*of*" has no business there. It is the name "*Ellicott*" that carries weight, not the name *of* Ellicott. In other words, it is the name of the *man*, not the name of the *name*. Again, the Professor says, "It follows, *as it seems to me* from these facts, that it is, *to say the least*, probable that the lost Order in Council, *if there ever were such an Order*, was permissive rather than compulsory." Here we have in one short sentence three parenthetical clauses besides an error in grammar! "If there ever *were* such an Order" should be, "If there ever *was* such an Order," because "the subjunctive mood in English is not used with propriety when we speak of that which is *past*." There are other errors in the Professor's paper, *e.g.*, "*should*" for "*would*," "*though*" for "*if*," "*either*" for "*each*," &c.; but I pass on to remark that, of those scholars whose names he mentions, the two who have the best reputation for a knowledge of the English language, namely, Archbishop Trench and Dr. Angus, were more frequently absent than present at the meetings of the Revision

Committee; indeed, the former was present only sixty-three times out of four hundred and seven; nor was any one of the rest, Bishop Ellicott excepted, present at three-fourths of the meetings. Therefore, from that cause as well, the English of the Revised New Testament has suffered.—Yours faithfully,

G. WASHINGTON MOON.

LETTER XXVII.

"Also," "Old" *or* "Of age," "Quick" *for* "Living." "*I* had *rather*," *for* "*I* would *rather*." "See-saw."

SIR,—It has been said that there is not, in the English language, one book in which the adverb "also" does not, by its position, qualify words to which it is not intended to apply.

The well-known commonness of this fault should have made the Revisers particularly desirous of rendering the Best of Books an exception to this just reproach. Yet, in 2 Cor. xi. 18, we read, "Seeing that many glory after the flesh, I will *glory also;*" it should be, "*I also*" will glory; as, indeed, it is in verse 16. The words, "I will glory also," would mean that the apostle would glory, in addition to doing something else; whereas his meaning was that, as others gloried, *he also* would glory.

Again, in verse 21, we read, "Whereinsoever any is bold, I am *bold also ;*" it should be, " *I also* am bold." The error is of frequent occurrence, and always has a tendency to make the writer's meaning ambiguous; it therefore is of very grave importance.

In Matt. x. 4, there is a list of the names of the apostles of our Lord; and it ends thus, " and Judas Iscariot, *who also* betrayed him." Any person who did not know the facts of the case would certainly infer, from these words, that Christ was betrayed by all the apostles, including of course Judas Iscariot, " *who also* betrayed him." The Revisers, after enumerating the eleven, should have said, "and Judas Iscariot *also, who* betrayed him."

If the Revisers of the New Testament had carried into practice the principle mentioned on page xiii. of their Preface, namely, to alter "obscure or ambiguous renderings into such as are clear and express in their import," the position of the adverb "*also*" would, in many passages, have been different.

While speaking of ambiguous renderings, I would call attention to 1 John v. 10, and ask the Revisers whether they do not think that some persons would be in doubt as to the meaning of the words, "He that believeth not God hath made him a liar;" and would have to ask, "Is it, 'He that believeth not—God hath made him a liar'? or is it, 'He that believeth not God—hath made Him a liar'?" I would recommend that, in the re-revision, the initial letters of the pronouns referring to God be printed in capitals.

In Luke viii. 42, it says that the daughter Jairus was about "twelve years *of age;*" but, in Mark v. 42, the Revisers say that she was "twelve years *old.*" Why this difference in the two narratives? In the Authorised Version it is, "she was *of the age* of twelve years;" and undoubtedly it is better to speak of a *young girl* as being a certain "*age*," than to speak of her as being "*old.*"

Another inconsistency is the Revisers' saying, in Luke viii. 42, that the little *girl* was about "twelve years *of age*," and, in the same book, Luke ii. 42, that the little *boy* was "twelve years *old*."

These are oversights which will be corrected; and I point them out for that purpose.

In the Revisers' Preface, p. xvii., they say, "We have never removed any archaisms, whether in structure or in words, except where we were persuaded either that the meaning of the words was not (it should be '*is* not') generally understood, or that the nature of the expression led to some misconception of the true sense of the passage."

I imagine, from their having altered "*quick*" to "*living*," in Heb. iv. 12, and "*quickening*" to "*life-giving*," in 1 Cor. xv. 45, that they realised the fact that the old meaning of "*quick*" and its derivatives is not generally understood. Why, then, has not this archaic word been eliminated from all the passages where it occurs?

Ask a poor unlettered man (and one of the glories of Christ's teaching was that the *poor* had the Gospel preached unto them), who are the "*quick*" of whom Christ is said to be the Judge (Acts x. 42), and notice what answer will be given you.

The Revisers have altered "*quickening spirit*" to "*life-giving spirit*," but have left unaltered the passage, "*It is the spirit that quickeneth.*" Compare 1 Cor. xv. 45, with John vi. 63.

"I *had* rather speak" is a very strange expression for the Revisers to have left in the New Testament; it should be, "I *would* rather speak." The error has arisen from the phrase, "*I'd* rather," being supposed to be a contraction of, not "I *would* rather," but of "I *had* rather." But the absurdity of the phrase, "I *had* rather speak," is evident on leaving out the adverb, "*rather;*" and that is a perfect test; for if it is correct to say, "I *had* rather speak," it must be correct to say, "I *had* speak!"

One of the most frequent errors in the Revised New Testament is the changing of the tense of the verb where there is no change of time in the incidents recorded. For example, in Matt. xix. 16–21, where the rich young man's conversation with Christ is recorded, we read, "And behold one came to him and *said* . . . he *saith* . . . Jesus *said* . . . The young man *saith*," and so on.

See also Luke xvi. 23–31, where we read of Lazarus that, "He lift*ed* up his eyes . . . and *seeth* . . . Abraham *said* . . . Abraham *saith* . . . Abraham *said*."

The same error occurs in John xx. 19–22, and 26, 27; and, indeed, on almost every page of the Gospel. In Mark xvi. 4, 5, we read respecting the resurrection, "And looking up they *see* that the stone is rolled back . . . and entering into the tomb they *saw* a young man." This truly is playing at "*see-saw*" with the verbs.—Yours faithfully,

G. WASHINGTON MOON.

LETTER XXVIII.

"Often" *for* "Frequent." "Shamefastness."
"Fallen" *for* "Falling."

SIR,—The use of the adverb "*often*" as an adjective is another error which the Revisers have sanctioned. It occurs in 1 Tim. v. 23, where we read, "Use a little wine for thy stomach's sake and thine *often* infirmities." It should be, "thy *frequent* infirmities." Adverbs, as is implied by the word itself, can qualify only verbs; nouns must be qualified by adjectives. Possibly the use of the word "*often*" has changed.

Dr. Johnson, in speaking of the word "*oftentimes*," says, "From the construction of this word (*often* and *times*), it is reasonable to believe that *oft* was once an adjective, of which *often* was the plural." But, whatever was once the case, it is certain that, in Bishop Lowth's time, more than a century ago, the use of "*often*" as an adjective was, as he says, "*wholly obsolete.*" See his "Introduction to English Grammar," p. 121.

Another obsolete word which the Revisers have used, probably at the instigation of Archbishop Trench, is "*shamefastness*" for "*shamefacedness;*" see 1 Tim. ii. 8, 9, "I desire . . . that women adorn themselves in modest apparel, with *shamefastness* and sobriety."

In the Preface, page xvii., as quoted previously, the Revisers say "We have never removed any archaisms, whether in structure or in words, except where we were persuaded either that the meaning of the words was not generally understood, or that the nature of the expression led to some misconception of the true sense of the passage." Now, it is just because the meaning of this word is not generally understood, and is therefore likely to lead to some misconception, that I object to it.

Of course, those of us who have read the first edition of the Authorised Version, published two hundred and seventy years ago, will recognise the word; but other persons, wondering what it means, will look in vain for it in the principal dictionaries. It is not in Johnson, Walker, Richardson, Ogilvie, Nuttall, Roget, or Latham, the word having so passed out of use as not to be even once mentioned by them. Why, then, have the Revisers inserted it?

Archbishop Trench considers that "*shamefacedness*," which is the form of the word in the Authorised Version now in use, is a corruption of "*shamefastness*" in the edition of 1611. But I am of opinion that, if the origin of the two words could be traced, "*shamefacedness*" would be found to be the earlier, and "*shamefästness*," and subsequently "*shamefästness*," a phonetic corruption of it.

The word "*shamefacedness*" is by no means modern. It occurs in Spenser's "Fairy Queen," the first part of which was published in 1591:—

"She is the fountain of your modesty,
You *shamefaced* are, but *shamefacedness* itself is she."

It is found in Sidney's writings also. He says, "Philocles, who blushing, and withal smiling, making *shamefacedness* pleasing."

The meaning of "*shamefacedness*" is obvious from these quotations; but the meaning of "*shamefastness*" will be a puzzle to many; and I can readily imagine the reading of the passage, "that women adorn themselves in modest apparel with shame*fastness* and sobriety," being followed by the remark, "Well, one sees a great deal of the *fastness* of women in these days; but, even when they are modestly dressed and sober, I never consider that their *fastness*, whether it is *shame-fastness* or any other kind of fastness, is any *adornment!* What does the passage mean?"

There is a very remarkable error in Luke x. 18, which, at the Newcastle Church Congress, was pointed out by Canon Evans. I had not noticed it; and for a very simple reason, namely, that, in the "Brevier 16mo" edition, a copy of which is the one that I use, the error does not exist. There the passage correctly reads as follows: "I beheld Satan *falling* as lightning from heaven;" but, in all the other editions of the Revised New Testament, it is, "I beheld Satan *fallen* as lightning from heaven." Now, as this latter reading occurs in four out of the five editions issued by both the Oxford and the Cambridge press, I fear that it must be accepted as the true expression of the Revisers' meaning; especially as the one edition which differs from all the others is faulty in other respects; for instance, 1 Cor. iii. 5, reads thus, "What then is Apollos? and what is Paul? Ministers through whom ye Lord believed; and each as the gave to him." The word "Lord" has been put after "ye," instead of after "the."

Accepting, then,' the weight of evidence in favour of "*fallen*," what a strange statement we have! "I beheld Satan *fallen* as lightning from heaven." This may mean either, "I beheld Satan fallen, as lightning from heaven;"

or, "I beheld Satan, fallen as lightning from heaven." The former idea is one of exceeding sublimity, "I beheld Satan in his fallen state, still like lightning from heaven!" But Canon Evans adopts the latter reading, and logically says, "If it is correct to say, 'I saw Satan fall like lightning,' it must also be correct to say, 'I saw lightning fall.' By a parity of reasoning, if it is correct to say, 'I beheld Satan fallen as lightning,' it must also be correct to say, 'I beheld lightning fallen.' But we cannot see lightning fallen; we can see it fall, but '*fallen*' we cannot see it." The only likeness, therefore, which can exist between "*lightning fallen*" and Satan, is that both are invisible.—Yours faithfully,

G. WASHINGTON MOON.

LETTER XXIX.

CONCLUSION.

Sir,—I have not said anything respecting the style of the language in the Revised New Testament. To take up that subject would be to extend these criticisms to what would, I fear, be considered a wearisome length. I will therefore reprint in parallel columns, merely one passage, the opening words of the Epistle to the Hebrews, and leave them to tell their own tale:—

AUTHORISED VERSION.	REVISED VERSION.
God, who at sundry times and in divers manners, spake in time past unto the fathers by the prophets,	God, having of old time spoken unto the fathers in the prophets by divers portions and in divers manners,
Hath in these last days spoken unto us by his Son.	hath at the end of these days spoken unto us in his Son.

Originally I purposed to point out some of

the improvements which the Revisers have made in the language of the New Testament, but I leave that for the present, and I also pass over many errors which still need correction. Perhaps I may, at some future time, resume the work; for, that there are many other errors, I need not say; any person conversant with English grammar must know that. Enough, however, has been said to show that although the Revisers have rendered essential service to the English-speaking peoples in all parts of the world, by making them better acquainted with the literal signification of the Greek, they are still left without such a version of the Sacred Scriptures as is worthy of their noble native language, and worthy of the glorious truths of Divine love.

By all means let the Revised Version be preserved for reference, but let there be based upon it another version for public reading in churches; one which, while adhering faithfully to the spirit and meaning of the Divine revelation, shall embody and give forth that meaning in all the soul-stirring music and rhythm of which words are capable.

There is scope in the varied themes of the Word of God for the grandest organ-utterances of language; and these, bearing those themes, should peal through the mighty cathedral of the world, in tones which could not but thrill with responsive vibrations the throbbing hearts of its many million worshippers.

On the reading of such a version, blessed by the Holy Spirit of God, they would tremble under the rolling thunder of its awful denunciations of hypocrisy; melt into gushing tearfulness of repentance beneath its gracious offers of mercy; and, in their depths of godly sorrow, would hear so tender a voice speaking to them in pitying accents of forgiveness that, influenced by those wondrous words of love, they would in spirit rise as on angels' wings of ecstasy to heaven, and adoringly bow in unutterable gratitude before the throne of the Most High.—Yours faithfully,

G. WASHINGTON MOON.

www.ingramcontent.com/pod-product-compliance
Lightning Source LLC
Chambersburg PA
CBHW030313170426
43202CB00009B/990